HOW TO ROCK YOUR LIFE

Maintain the Magic of Live Music in Your Everyday Experience

by Taraleigh Weathers

Foreword by Dead & Company Bassist Oteil Burbridge

BALBOA
PRESS

A DIVISION OF HAY HOUSE

Balboa Press books may be ordered through booksellers or by contacting:

Balboa Press
A Division of Hay House
1663 Liberty Drive
Bloomington, IN 47403
www.balboapress.com
1 (877) 407-4847

Because of the dynamic nature of the Internet, any web addresses or links contained in this book may have changed since publication and may no longer be valid. The views expressed in this work are solely those of the author and do not necessarily reflect the views of the publisher, and the publisher hereby disclaims any responsibility for them.

The author of this book does not dispense medical advice or prescribe the use of any technique as a form of treatment for physical, emotional, or medical problems without the advice of a physician, either directly or indirectly. The intent of the author is only to offer information of a general nature to help you in your quest for emotional and spiritual well-being. In the event you use any of the information in this book for yourself, which is your constitutional right, the author and the publisher assume no responsibility for your actions.

Any people depicted in stock imagery provided by Thinkstock are models, and such images are being used for illustrative purposes only.
Certain stock imagery © Thinkstock.

Print information available on the last page.

ISBN: 978-1-5043-5594-0 (sc)
ISBN: 978-1-5043-5596-4 (hc)
ISBN: 978-1-5043-5595-7 (e)

Library of Congress Control Number: 2016906417

Balboa Press rev. date: 01/18/2018

Dear Live Music Lovin Humans,

I dedicate this book to you. My dream is that you connect with the life experiences and struggles I unabashedly share with you so you can learn from my mistakes and soar like the magnificent mongoose you were meant to be. I hope that my vulnerable stories paired with my recommendations inspire you to rock your life before, during and after the show.

The magic in me sees the magic in you,

CONTENTS

FOREWORD

By Oteil Burbridge: Dead & Company Bassist

When I first met Taraleigh, it was at this festival called Jungle Jam that I try to attend every year in Costa Rica. They had yoga classes there, and we ended up in the same class a few times. Since both of us are pretty outgoing, it didn't take us long to talk, and we realized that we were both in the coolest part of our lives so far. If you're lucky enough to be aware that the coolest part of your life is happening right now, then you will find yourself most grateful and happy. In the past, my problem was that I was living the coolest part of my life many times and didn't fully realize it.

Of course, it's the worst parts of your life that really make you aware of how cool the good parts are. Taraleigh and I, as with many others, had been through some really bad stuff and came out on the other side. Sometimes it feels like it's happening to you instead of for you, and it's easy to play the victim. It's the stuff that we do or let happen to ourselves that Taraleigh and I talk about a lot. That's the stuff that fascinates me. We want to know why we fall into that trap.

Why do we get into negative patterns? Are we just made that way? Is it fear? If so, then what are we afraid of? And why are we afraid of it? I'm always wondering about the why.

I think we also share an awareness that life is potentially really short. Obviously, it could be really long too, but that's no guarantee. Hell, a really long life is ultimately just as bad if things are always crappy! Taraleigh and I both tend to want to confront and sort out the things that are not in harmony with where we are. Sometimes our misery is found in just going along with other people's visions of our lives. Sometimes just going with the flow is exactly the wrong thing to do. The key is being able to discern the difference. I'm sure that a motto we both live by is "The time is now."

I went from feeling like I was incapable of ever feeling at peace inside to thinking that it was possible but would probably take a really long time. After watching a small bunch of people die very early in life, I realized that I better make it happen immediately. When you have that fire under your ass, other people who have it too stick out to you. We might as well have our foreheads painted with some distinguishing mark. By the way, if you haven't met her yet, Taraleigh has a huge, sequined, sparkly mark on her forehead. Actually, it's probably a full-blown headdress! You can't miss her.

Intentional happiness might be a good way to describe it. To some, that may seem fake, but I don't think that's true. What if your favorite thing was a certain type of food and you were told by your doctor that you needed to stop eating it? I would go out that night and get it made for me by a gourmet chef, because it was going to be the last time. I would intentionally savor that meal more than I would if I knew I could have it any time I wanted it. This is how we both try to

approach life now. The time to do your bucket list is now, not right before you're about to die!

Taraleigh can't help but want to scream that to the world.

We certainly are not in control of everything. Thank God! But we have more influence over our consciousness than we might realize. And if we have that fire under our ass and even intermittent bravery, we can get a lot closer to happiness than we previously thought. We both believe that our consciousness is the most powerful thing on the planet, for better and for worse.

We want it to be for the better. The creative power of intention, visualization, action, prayer, patience, quietude, hoping, loving, listening, letting go, being honest with yourself, curiosity, openness, and forgiveness is boundless.

Taraleigh sees this so clearly. She sees that happiness is also a decision and not just a feeling. Happiness can be a lot like chocolate; you know it's there, but it's not gonna just come to you.

Luckily, we know a few places we can find it. We have to get off our asses and go get it, and be willing and able to pay for it. Of course sometimes someone you love will put some by your bedside, and when you wake up, there it is. That costs something too, though.

Taraleigh's not wasting time anymore. And when it looks like she is, believe me, she's not. She's just savoring.

WHY I WROTE THIS BOOK

I was fidgeting nervously in my seat trying to gather up the courage to do something I'd been waiting all year to do. I distracted myself by making it my mission to guess every single object that was occupying my desk by touch. My fingers gently grazed over my trapper keeper. Next I discovered the coolest pen I ever owned that I received as an early birthday present from my best friend. It had five different color options, all of them neon. Woah! I know. I grasped my hand tightly around my wooden ruler, taking notice of every ding and scratch in it. My recorder, whose mouth piece was extremely sticky from my saliva, was the next item in my desk before ewwwwww! Unfortunately I just found the piece of week old chewing gum I sneakily took out of my mouth when I suspected my teacher was onto my rebellion and shoved it in the back corner of my desk.

Grossed out by my most recent find, I abruptly aborted my mission. Running out of stuff to distract me, I noticed heat was building in my body starting from my head and moving down. Was it because of the super thick corduroy jumper my mom picked out for me to wear or was it the wool turtleneck sweater that I just realized was getting itchier by the second? Could the heat be coming from my feet that were throbbing in my favorite turquoise high top Converse All-Star sneakers that I refused to admit that I'd outgrown?

None of those things were the culprit. I was totally freaking myself out about what I was about to do. I had been avoiding it since the first day of school.

No wonder I was so terrified. My teacher was the kind of woman you would spontaneously combust from feeling too much fear at one time if you found yourself alone with her in a dark alley. Shaking like a leaf, I slowly and sheepishly raised my hand. It was easy for me to hide because I was so physically small and was seated behind the tallest boy in our class. My teacher spotted my adorable pig-tailed head and called my name. Immediately all eyes were glued on me. Time slowed down and I looked at the door, formulating an escape plan in my head. I could totally sliver out the door and make my way into the hallway, run past the office, out the main door and into the woods where I would build a little hut out of twigs and spend the rest of my life and never be seen again. Abruptly I was pulled out of my fantasy by my teacher's louder than thunder voice. Her tone getting more intense by the minute, my teacher asked me again what I wanted. I panicked and pulled my hand down as fast as I could, while sinking lower and lower into my seat and attempting to make my teeny-tiny body even tinier.

My teacher sternly asked again, "Tara, WHAT do you WANT?"

I mumbled as loud as a mouse trying to sneak some cheese when a cat is lurking around the corner, "I want to lead the pledge of allegiance." She couldn't hear me, and instead of lovingly coaxing me to use my voice, she started furiously screaming at me, hands flailing and all. The kids in my class did what kids do and giggled and pointed at the person who was on the receiving end of the teacher's wrath. My name was feverishly scratched onto the chalkboard for the day, which to me felt like all eternity. In second grade, a name on the board is the ultimate shame.

That experience was so life shatteringly traumatic for shy little second grade me. I came up with a bunch of "truths" that day, which I believed for years to protect myself from anything like that ever happening to me again.

I believed that if I spoke up, I would get laughed at. I decided I was stupid and should keep quiet in fear of getting ridiculed. I shied away from the spotlight because it was a place of shame and embarrassment. After that blip in time all those years ago, I lurked in the shadows hoping no one would find me in my hiding spot.

As an adult, the repercussions of that day still haunted me. I was asked to be a speaker for various events and I would work myself into such a frantic tizzy that I would violently throw up. I even found myself on my hands and knees puking the night before my wedding because I was terrified to read my vows in front of my loving friends and family. As it manifested in all of my relationships, I let men, so-called friends, co-workers, bosses and roommates walk all over me. In my twenties, I found myself in a four-year, emotionally and physically abusive relationship that I couldn't find the courage to leave.

Over time I grew to adore public speaking and, once I was actually doing it, I felt like I was home. I belonged there, yet I continued to freak myself out beforehand. Finally, after what felt like my thousandth puking episode, I knew I had to do something because what I was doing wasn't working.

My first course of action was to forgive the shy-adorable-innocent little second grader that still lives inside of me. She was doing the best she could with the life experience she had on that day when she was so brave even to raise her hand.

Next, I was to forgive myself for buying into those beliefs that dimmed my light for so long because I was doing the best I could with the life experience I had so far.

The third course of action was to forgive my teacher and the kids who laughed at me. They were doing the best they could with the life experience they had so far, too.

My fourth course of action was to write some new and improved beliefs based on my new mantras, which are, "I was put on this planet to shine just like everyone else," "My voice matters," and "I speak my truth from a place of love without attachment to how it will be perceived by others."

To seal the deal of my new truths, not too long ago I visited a second grade classroom and shared my story with the wildly excitable kids. I saw myself in each of their sweet, innocent little eyes and couldn't imagine not wanting to absorb every word that came out of their magical tiny mouths. After sharing my story and leading the pledge for the group, a little boy in corduroy overalls with bushy hair and thick black rimmed glasses confidently approached me. I could tell right away he was wise beyond his years. He said matter of factly, "Taraleigh. When I have to speak in front of my class I get nervous too. I excuse myself to the bathroom, look at myself in the mirror and say, 'You're awesome!' You should do that too because I think you're just as awesome as me."

You're right little man!

Since then I have been speaking out in all kinds of ways, including writing this book.

Do you have a second grader inside of you, still upset about not speaking up? Or a seventh grader who didn't get asked to the dance? Or who got picked on, bullied, or not chosen to be on a team in gym class? It's time to give your love to that little one who still lives within you. It's time to acknowledge that some bad stuff has happened along the journey. I'm not about putting sparkles on top of poop. You'll learn so much in this book about how to deal with all your stuff and sometimes it won't be all rainbows and unicorns.

I have A LOT to say about all of that!

You enjoy my book.

A Few Reasons You Should Keep on Reading

If you close this book now, the next time you use a port-o-potty at a festival, you will fall in. Just kidding!

> "The constitution only guarantees the American people the right to the pursuit of happiness. You have to catch it yourself."
>
> ~Benjamin Franklin

It's a freakin crazy planet we call home. Bad things have been happening all over the world all along. Right now, someone is raping, pillaging, lying, cheating, or stealing. Someone is getting ridiculed just for being different. People are getting sick, finding out they're sick, and some are taking their last breaths here on earth. It's easy to get stuck in the whirlwind of fear and have it take the reins over your thoughts.

But, the world has also always been a beautiful place, too. Your focus might be drawn to what's wrong with the human race, but realize that right now, all kinds of acts of love and kindness are being committed. People are having babies, beating diseases, falling in love, writing music, creating art, and exploring new places as you are reading these words.

I have fallen prey to thinking everyone is bad and out to steal from me, lie to me, hate on me, exclude me, and take advantage of me. My ego and my deep dark fears have told me many things like that, but they are not where the truth lies. The truth hangs out in my heart. Whenever I get caught up in victimhood, I always ask my heart what's up and the answer is always the same.

Love, love, love and then love a little more.

I know it ain't always easy, but the more you flex your love muscle, the stronger it will get. The stronger it gets the more your world will shift from shit to sparkles.

There's a documentary called *Happiness Is*. Pouring myself a steaming cup of chamomile tea, I melted into the cushions of my couch, wrapped myself up like a burrito in my luxurious fuzzy blanket, and focused all of my attention on the movie. Truth bombs were dropped all over my living room that evening.

Fifty percent of your happiness is determined by genetics. Some people are more genetically predisposed to happiness than others. If you are someone who finds it difficult to be happy, don't worry. I've got good news for you. Society and the media are geniuses at tricking us into believing that the more stuff we have and the more we consume, the more fulfilled we will feel, leaving us thinking that most of our happiness is based on our circumstances. Guess what the research found? Only 10 percent of your happiness is based on circumstances. So what about the other 40 percent? It comes from intentional behavior, and that is what this book is all about!

The main inspiration for this book came to me at a music festival. Actually, most of my greatest ideas happen on the concert field. It probably has something to do with the fact that I'm obsessed with live music, and anywhere it's happening is my happy place. When I'm at a show, I experience so much joy. I let loose and dance my heart out like everyone's watching, but I don't care. I surround myself with new and old friends. I can be found in the crowd yelling "Woo!" and fist pumping, spinning in circles, performing high kicks, busting out the running man, bopping my head, dressed head to toe in sparkles and feathers, while giving and receiving as many hugs as I possibly can. I smile so much my face muscles feel sore the next day.

In the past, the only time I felt comfortable in my skin was when I was knee deep in a live music experience. The moment the band plays their first note, I exhale out all of the stresses that I carry with me. All judgement instantly evaporates into the patchouli-filled air as I start to notice other weirdos just like me. No one attempts to hide their weird, because why would you? Everyone's uniqueness is celebrated and honored there.

This is why I've seen the bands Phish and Moe. over 100 times and why I plan my vacations and events around festival and tour schedules. My people (aka my tribe of weirdos) flock there and I always feel safe to let my freak flag fly when I am around them. Not too long ago, I was afraid to let that part of me out when I was at home. I totally smothered the wildest expression of my authentic self and I felt like I was suffocating.

I didn't go from wearing khakis to sparkles on everything overnight. I like to say I was an authentic self flasher. Now you see the real me. Now you don't. There was a secret happening below the surface; I almost always had tie-dyed underwear hiding beneath my adulting costume, and during my lunch break I could be found in a bathroom stall having a raging dance party to the Grateful Dead on my iPod.

The more I flashed my true self and was pleasantly surprised that I didn't just straight up keel over and die, the happier I felt. Even though I would get uncomfortably stared at for my outfit choices and honked and pointed at when I was dancing down the street, I started to notice that I didn't care, because my personal bliss was worth the risk of looking strange to the world.

The thing is, I know you want to be happy.

Not the kind of happy where you say one thing but do something else. Not putting on a pair of ill-fitting tight pants and telling yourself you look and feel good in them anyway. Not the kind of happy that wears a mask to hide what's really going on underneath it.

I'm talking about the real stuff.

Maybe you've read a million self-help books, and you still aren't feeling happy. I feel ya big time. I've read them all. They all basically say the same things, but in the unique voice of the author. Some I've resonated with and others I didn't. If you are resonating with my words right now, flip the page and keep reading.

1

CONSCIOUSLY INFUSE THE LIVE MUSIC MAGIC INTO YOUR EVERYDAY EXPERIENCE

"I would not get up
I would dance on my back
Throw my legs up in the air like I don't care
Then wave them side to side
Then I'd bust into a windmill then right into a backspin."

Tweaker By The Speaker by Keller Williams

After college, I felt the pressure from society and my family to get off Phish tour, get a real job and act like a grown-up. I resorted to spending my time the same way most of my friends were: stressing out about money, boyfriends, and friend dramas, all while pursuing jobs that weren't aligned with their desires. But they 'paid the bills!'

During that dark time in my life, I got so caught up in the adulting tornado that I totally forgot something that was essential for real success. I looked everywhere outside of me for it, to no avail. I often wondered, "Where did all the joy go?" I knew it had to be lurking somewhere under the surface and I was determined to find it.

So I did what any responsible adult would do. I started to play more and I went to as many live music shows as I possibly could.

As a wildly hyper youngster, I spent my care-free childhood days dressed in outfits that weren't supposed to go together that I always paired with mismatched neon colored socks. Jumping as high as I could on my mini trampoline, sliding down my stairs on an old mattress, riding bikes all over town with the neighborhood kids, choreographing full on dance routines with my sister in my yard and doing other blissful kid-like fun activities was how I expressed myself.

As an adult, I wondered how I could add a little of that childlike freedom into my daily responsibilities. I allowed myself to play at festivals, but when I came home, it was like all the fun abruptly ended and the real life suckiness set in. What if singing in the shower, dressing up in a tutu and flower a crown when cleaning the house, and adding dance breaks in the bathroom stall at work were all doable solutions for my no-fun problem? I tried it and something very interesting started happening. Not only were my spirits lifted all around, but I found myself way more productive, motivated, successful, and abundant. Playing wasn't a selfish waste of time at all like I had originally thought because what my playtime did for me was to make me be playfully productive.

Growing up and being the innocent impressionable child I was, I was told many things by friends, family, and society, such as:

"You must work yourself to the bone to be successful."

"Work isn't supposed to be enjoyable; it's just something you must do."

"There's no time for fun now. If you can muster up the energy you can do it at night, on the weekends, and when you retire."

What I've found out through experiencing the world in my own unique way is that none of those things are true for me. When I started to rebel against the status quo, my world was rocked to the core, and everything I ever believed was challenged. You must work hard, that part is true, but instead of pushing against the resistance and eventually burning out, move toward the direction of the flow and allow the work to feel more effortless. Loving what you do and actually enjoying it, you'll have way more energy to put into it than if you hate it. That's the pathway that will lead you to true sustainable success. Don't wait until you're retired to have fun, because who knows if you'll make it to retirement anyway.

Going to shows are just as important to your health as drinking enough water is.

If you don't make time for activities that leave you feeling good a priority in your life, eventually, over time, you'll hit rock bottom and get your bootylicious backside handed to you on a platter. Mine has been served to me on that platter so many times that I don't have enough fingers and toes to count them on.

Second grade, pretty bad. Abusive boyfriend in my twenties, crushing. Countless jobs that sucked the soul out of me, not fun. Professional dancer-ending physical injury, thought it was the end of the world. The silver lining is when you hit rock bottom, there's nowhere to go but up.

Even though I wish I could take you in my arms and protect you so you never have to experience any pain, I can't do that for you. My hope is that you take all the tools I give you in this book, put them into practice, and rock your life.

When your life is rockin, it may trigger some people in your life. Our culture doesn't really celebrate happiness and, because of this, most adults have a really hard time admitting that they desire to be (insert gasp here) happy. They'll easily give you sympathy when things go wrong and revel in the darkness with you. Even on your birthday, you'll get more likes on social media if you say how you had the worst day ever than if you tell everyone how awesome your life is.

On my Facebook page I found these words from a man I didn't know: "You really love yourself, huh?" followed by a rant about how self-centered, narcissistic, and arrogant I was. Second guessing myself and my awesomeness, I thought, "No I don't! I'm not that great." But then I heard my mind chatter and what it was really saying and I didn't like it one bit. Actually, he was right. I really do love myself, and it's really sad that loving myself is looked at by our society as a negative thing. After I realized the truth, I responded, "Yes, I do love myself. Thank you for the reminder."

I end my emails with: The magic in me sees the magic in you. When you allow yourself to see the beauty in yourself, you allow others to see it in themselves too. If your light is hiding under a whole bunch of layers of gunk right now, let's make a pathway for your shine to get to the surface just like it did when you were a bright eyed baby. Along the journey, you're bound to hit a crossroad where you'll have to decide which way you want to go. With what I've laid out for you in this book, you'll have everything you need to choose the correct direction. Spoiler alert: Whichever way feels more alive, choose that one.

Note: Please read the following paragraph as if you're Prince reciting the introduction to his hit song, *Let's Go Crazy*.

Dearly beloved, we are gathered here today to get through this thing called "life." Electric word, life. It means forever and that's a mighty long time, but I'm here to tell you, there's something else; the Sweet Life. A world of never ending happiness. You can always see the sun, day or night. So ditch your party pooper habits, you know the ones, Mr. Nothing-Ever-Goes-Right. And if anyone tries to bring you down, go crazy. Woo!

Don't Be a Party-Pooper. Here's how to Ditch Those Nasty Habits:

- **Give up the need to always be right.** In the scheme of things, does it really matter if you're right or not? Try being open to others' thoughts and opinions.
- **Let go of the need to control everyone and everything**. You can't do it no matter how hard you try, and more than likely it'll leave you stressed out, anxious, in a constant state of worry, and you might even feel a sense of being even more out of control.
- **Release the urge to blame others for how sucky your life is**. The only person responsible for how you feel about your life, is you. When you point your finger at someone, three fingers are pointing back at you.
- **Stop talking trash about yourself.**
- **Crush the belief that you're entitled to only so much happiness, wealth, or love.**
- **Fight the urge to complain.** Whining about a situation, person, or event doesn't change the situation, person, or event. The situation is a fact, but it's how you choose to react to it that makes all the difference. The more you complain, the more things you'll find to complain about, and the more you will find yourself bonding with unhappy people who also complain. It's a trap!
- **Squash the need to constantly impress others.** What anyone else thinks about you is none of your business.

- **Embrace change**. Change is the one thing in your life you can count on to always be there. You can't avoid it from happening so you might as well go with it.
- **Don't allow fear to stop you**. Fear is a good thing because without it you would more than likely be dead. There are two different types of fear though. Being chased by a tiger fear and roller coaster fear. When your life is actually in danger (like when a tiger is chasing you), and you need to run to survive, that is the first type. The second is when it feels scary (like going on a roller coaster), but there's little to no chance of death. They physically feel the same in your body, but they're way different. If your life isn't threatened, feel that fear and go for it anyway.
- **Stop making excuses about why you can't do things.** I've heard them all, used them all, and they're all lame. Don't buy into the lies. They might feel real, but they aren't real.
- **Don't allow your past to rule your present.** If you focus too much on what's in the rear view mirror, you'll crash.
- **Let go of grudges.** Forgiveness and compassion is where the true magic lies. The only person suffering from not doing so is you.
- **Listen to your favorite songs.** It's almost impossible to be a party-pooper when your favorite song is bumpin in your ears.

Always Consult Your Ninety-Year-Old Self

An article by Bronnie Ware, a nurse who worked in palliative care with patients during their last few weeks of life, struck a chord with me. She found the top five regrets of the dying (and wrote a book about it called *The Top Five Regrets of the Dying: A Life Transformed by the Dearly Departing*.)

Here are the top five regrets of the dying:

I wish I'd had the courage to live a life true to myself, not the life others expected of me.

I wish I hadn't worked so hard.

I wish I'd had the courage to express my feelings.

I wish I had stayed in touch with my friends.

I wish that I had let myself be happier.

I wish I experienced more live music (this one isn't from Bronnie's book, but I felt that for this book, it must be added).

You see, everyone has a desire to live a sweet life. Some just don't realize it until the last few weeks of their lives.

My long-time friend Cora called me in a panic one day. She had felt this strong desire to go to Peru ever since she could remember. In fact, when Cora's grandmother was on her deathbed, she shared how she had always wanted to travel there. Cora promised her grandmother that she would take that trip to Peru one day, since her grandmother would never get to. A couple of weeks prior, Cora had been presented with the perfect opportunity to take that trip. At first she was like, "I'm in!" Then her brain started questioning everything. "Who are you to be taking this much time off of work?" "You are being selfish." "Can you even afford this?"

Her heart was a clear yes, but her mind was questioning it, so I told her to step into her ninety-year-old self. I asked, "What would you say to yourself right now?"

Without hesitation, Cora said, "Go to Peru, you weiner head!"

The elder within us is so smart and wise, and, sometimes, a little snarky.

I haven't been ninety yet (at least not in this lifetime), but I learn a lot from consulting the ninety-year-old within me. She's personally responsible for my time on Phish tour, booking my spot on Jam

Cruise, and jumping at the chance to join one of my friends at Coachella. Here's some of the wisdom she's dropped on me:

Don't let money or the 'right time' hold you back from what's really important to you. I regret spending money on that epic, life changing trip. (Said no one, ever!) This isn't a permission slip to spend money frivolously; just listen to your heart and don't wait for the "perfect" time to go for it, because there's never a "perfect" time.

Appreciate those you love. Go out of your way to love your loved ones up. You don't know how long they will be with you, so the time is now.

Make an effort to stay connected with friends.

Don't work too much. You probably don't want to be remembered as someone who was an absent mother/father/friend/spouse because they worked eighty hours a week.

Have fun! Life's too short not to. Maybe not all day, every day, but allow yourself to have a little fun on a daily basis.

Take care of yourself now. Actions you take when you're younger have a huge effect on how you'll feel when you're older.

Dance like everyone's watching, but you don't care. Everyone has an opinion and you're more than likely getting judged, so you might as well give em something to talk about.

Live in the moment and feel good about your choices. YOLO (You only live once) is a popular saying with the kids these days, and it's true. You do only live once (at least in this lifetime, depending on your beliefs), but what that saying doesn't mean is that you should sleep with that stranger, wolf down a triple cheeseburger at 2:00 a.m., and get crazy wasted on drugs and alcohol. You only live once, but the goal is to wake up tomorrow feeling good about the choices you made.

"Stuff" isn't important. People and your time are. The blissful summer day you raged the parking lot before the big show with your best buds, that holiday you got to spend with your grandpa before he passed away, or helping your kids with their art project are all more valuable than any chatzky money can buy.

Go see live music.

Infuse Live Music Magic Into Your Everyday Experience

I used to chase the feelings I felt when I was having a live music experience all over the country for just one more taste of the good stuff. Actually, I still travel far and wide to rock out to my favorite bands, but now-a-days there is a big difference. The biggest change I made, was instead of pissing away the present moment waiting for the next show to let the wildest expression of my authentic self out, I let her out (little by little) everyday, all the time, and in everything I did.

Identifying what those feelings were in the first place was where I started. For me, I felt free, wild, magical, in the flow, and blissed out. After naming the feelings, I conjured up a plan to start to feel them on a daily basis.

I started throwing myself mini-festivals throughout the day. At my mini-festival, there was always music and my body would never stay still. Whenever possible, there was biodegradable glitter, patchouli, sparkly clothing, and tie-dye. I used to carry a flower crown in my purse for the occasion. My favorite venues were the shower, my car, bathroom stalls, the sidewalk, and my closet.

Some more of my top activities that bring out those feelings are writing in my journal, going for a walk, hiking and yoga. I give so many more examples in Chapter 4: Achieve Self-Care Superhero Status.

Why Having a Life Sponsor Is Essential and How to Choose Yours

This is a story toward the path of sobriety about my friend, Mike T, who is a recovering alcoholic.

Holding a cold cup of black coffee in his hand that he was too distracted to drink, he was filled with equal parts anxiety and hope. His life had fallen apart all around him, so he decided he was going to get sober. The way he was going to stick with it and stay that way was to go to Alcoholics Anonymous. About to meet with his sponsor for the first time, he wondered how that person would truly help him. Being at the very beginning of his road to recovery, not picking up the bottle again seemed like an impossible mission. Stepping into unknown territory, he met with his sponsor, and together they went through the twelve steps laid out in the program. Each week his sponsor checked in with him to see how he was doing. By talking with his sponsor, he felt even more invested in himself and in his sobriety because someone was there to hold him accountable for his actions.

Doing this work and making changes about what he didn't like within himself and his life, things started to shift internally for Mike. He felt safe with and fully trusted his sponsor to not only check in with him when things were going great, but, even more importantly, when things weren't. The shoulder he needed to lean on as he learned how to live sober (which he didn't know how to do on his own) was always there for him.

When Mike was looking for his ideal sponsor, he gave me some tips that can be applied to anyone wanting to improve their life.

He said, "You must find someone who has been through what you've been through, who knows more than you do right now, and who is living life the way you want to live it. There must be some sort of connection, a knowing that you can trust them, and they must be willing to hold you accountable and give you tough love no matter what."

"Sponsors can change, based on how you grow and evolve. When I work with a sponsor, I feel better than when I don't. If you outgrow your sponsor, find another one," Mike shared.

Most people who are successful with their sobriety are participating in sponsorship.

People in AA are committed to their sobriety. If you're committed to rocking your life, you'll need a sponsor too.

When you pick your Life Sponsor, look for someone who's been through what you've been through, who knows more than you do right now, who is living life the way you want to live it, will challenge you, is willing to give you a swift kick in your tushie when you need one, and is a live music fanatic.

Not everyone you ask will say yes to wanting to take on the task of being your sponsor. There are so many reasons one would say no to such an undertaking, so remember that it's not personal if someone doesn't want to do it. Make a list of at least three ideal sponsors just in case you encounter such an obstacle.

Without my Life Sponsors, I would be a straight up disaster zone. Deciding that I needed one, I reached out to a woman who I saw speak at a conference. She was confident, authentic, serious, silly and successful. What she had was something I wanted. I was so nervous to talk to her because I thought she was so amazing. Little did I know, she saw me speak at that same conference and felt the same way about me as I felt about her. After a phone call, we knew right away that we would be each other's Life Sponsors. We each had qualities that the other desired. After a couple of months of sponsorship with each other, another sponsorship duo contacted us asking if we wanted to partner up with them too. The Unicorn Sisterheart was born (aka my Life Sponsors), and we talk for two hours every month. On top of that, we have an agreement that we call 1-800-dial-a-unicorn, which means if one of us needs a little extra in-the-moment support, we can text the group and whoever is available offers up their support on the spot.

Those three women hold me accountable, don't buy into any excuses I give them, are there for me when I'm freaking out, and give me a swift kick in my sweet ass when I need it. They're my biggest cheerleaders. When they started sponsoring me, I was very clear with what I was looking for. Every six months, we check in with each other, talk about what's working and what could be better and choose whether we want to move forward together.

Suggested Listening:

Sparkle by Phish
Those Were The Days by Mary Hopkin
YOLO by The Lonely Island featuring Adam Levine
Fresh Street by Zach Deputy
My Girl by The Temptations
Beautiful Day by Spafford
Songbird by Ryan Montbleau

ROCK THE MAGIC!

What are your party pooper habits?

Which ones are you going to ditch? Put them in the trash.

How do you feel when you're experiencing live music? List three to five feelings.

What do you do at your mini-festivals to evoke those feelings?

What venues are you going to throw mini-festivals at?

Choose your Life Sponsor.

Who in your world pops your proverbial champagne cork? (Meaning, they're an amazing person who inspires you, would help you move in the direction of your dreams, and are open to you picking their brain that you can enroll as your sponsor?)

Once you come up with around three bees knees people, start with your favorite person and ask them if they'd like to be your Life Sponsor. If they say no, move to the next person in line.

When someone says yes, set up a virtual or in-person play date.

Play date ideas:

Meet at a tea shop or have virtual tea together and talk about your dreams and how you can playfully move towards them.

Have a virtual or live hula hoop or dance party. While you're shaking your groove thing you can come up with your sponsorship plan.

Watch an inspirational video together and talk about how you can infuse a little (or a lot) of that into your life. Not sure where to find videos? Try TedTalks, Hay House, or search inspirational videos on YouTube.

List your own play date ideas:

Writing Prompt

Write a letter to your present-day self from your ninety-year-old self.

Reflections:

2

GET HIGH

"I'd had a bad night
I mean a night so bad, I thought I was king of the world
And I drank 'til daylight
I mean I never stopped once until my hands finally fell
And I fought my daytime self with a mighty dose of,
"Hey, look at night time me!"
And I never do win that battle, but I fight it over and
over and over it seems"

75 and Sunny by Ryan Montbleau

One of my heroes, Dr. Wayne Dyer said this in his book *The Power of Intention*:

"What you may fail to see inside is a result of how you choose to process everything and everyone in your world. You project onto the world what you see inside, and you fail to project into the world what you fail to see inside. If you knew that you were an expression of the universal spirit of intention, that's what you'd see. You'd raise your energy level beyond any possibility of encumbrances to your connection to the power of intention. It is only discord acting within your own feelings that will ever deprive you of every good thing that life holds for you! If you understand this simple observation, you'll curb interferences to intention."

Every thought or feeling has a vibration that can be measured. Science can back that shit up! The reason you want to raise these vibrations is so you become high enough to connect to the power of intention. It's the vibration of love where anything is possible, aka the sweet spot where you experience the most joy and happiness and life feels easier (If you've attended a festival before, chances are you've gotten a taste of what it feels like to be in this vibration).

Warning: The following information I'm about to give you is an instruction manual on how to get super high. Proceed at full speed.

1. Become conscious of your thoughts. Every single thought that comes into your head has an impact. In the past I thought some really negative things and often found myself assuming the worst possible outcomes for many situations. I manifested unsavory experiences into my life that proved those thoughts were right.

Since I was so good at manifesting the stuff I didn't want into my life, I thought that maybe with a little shift to my thought pattern, I had the possibility to be just as successful getting what I truly wanted instead. Spending time building up my positive thought muscle, all of a sudden I started manifesting beautiful and magical things into my world.

You may not hop on the positive thought train for good overnight, or maybe you will. Sign up for the hypothetical positive thought gym and lift a one-pound positivity weight and build up from there until you become a bodybuilder.

Affirmations are awesome tools to use. Come up with a good one and place it in a spot where you'll notice it, like the corner of your mirror. Repeat yours at least three times every time you see it. You don't have to completely believe it for your affirmation to work. Look at yourself in the mirror, read it loud and proud (or quiet and proud depending on your home situation and the other beings that live in it), and then take a deep breath and feel it to be true in every cell in your body. Over time it will become your truth. An example of a good affirmation is:

"I am a vital part of this Universe. I am loved and valued as I love and value those around me. Every day I am stronger and more grateful for this beautiful life."

(A big thank you to my cuz-in-law Katie for sharing her personal affirmation with us.)

2. Meditate. Only have a minute? That's cool. Use that minute to be silent and present. I used to resist meditating with all my might. I was always super fidgety and my mind was constantly going bonkers with all the thoughts running through it. I used to think meditation was used to shut down your thoughts, but it's not true. When you meditate, you observe your thoughts like clouds in the sky. When you find yourself stuck on a thought, bring your awareness to the breath coming in and out of your nose. Just like how you started off lifting a one-pound positive-thought weight, you can start lifting a one-pound meditation weight too, and before you know it, you will be a meditation heavyweight superstar.

3. Eat real food. If the food you consume is covered in pesticides, they will leave you feeling weakened because they vibrate low. On the low-vibration list are simple carbohydrates, dairy, refined sugars and processed foods. The high-vibe foods are organic fruits, veggies, and nuts. These rules aren't the end-all, be-all, since our biological make-ups are so different. Pay attention to how you feel immediately after eating and again two hours after. Keep a food journal for two weeks to see how what you're eating is affecting you.

Try this recipe!

High Vibe Smoothie

Ingredients:

1 banana

1 cup spinach

1 cup unsweetened non-dairy milk (coconut, almond, hemp, flax, rice)

2 tablespoons almond, cashew or peanut butter

1 tbsp pure maple syrup or honey

1/2 cup water

5 ice cubes

Directions:

Place all the ingredients in the blender.

Blend until smooth.

Drink.

And this one:

High As the Sky Ice Cream

Ingredients:

1 frozen banana (One banana per serving) Be sure to peel the banana prior to freezing.

Optional mix ins: blueberries, nuts, nut butters, cherries, strawberries and/or cacao nibs

Directions:

Add banana to food processor or blender and blend.

Scrape down the sides as needed and continue blend until smooth as a baby's butt. (Approximately 3 minutes)

Scoop into a bowl as you sing Shoop by Salt-n-Pepa.

If you like soft serve ice cream, enjoy this delicious treat right away. If you like it a little firmer (so many jokes!!!!), place it in an airtight freezer safe container and freeze for an hour or more while listening to the Tweezer Phish played in Stateline, Tahoe on July 31, 2013.

4. Just say no or practice moderation when it comes to drugs and alcohol. Getting an instant high and feeling like the king of the world in the moment may give the illusion of being vibrationally high, but unfortunately alcohol and almost all artificial drugs vibrate low. If your best buds partake in drug use, they probably spend time looking for drugs, hanging out with people who sell drugs, or pressure you into doing more drugs which is mega low vibe.

I've experimented with some pretty serious drugs in the past. I participated simply because I wanted to hang out with my friends and be on their level, and I didn't want to miss out on what I perceived to be "all the fun." Over time I realized that I never really missed out on that much fun. Once I really started working on raising my vibration, I found that I didn't need those drugs to feel high because I naturally felt like what everyone was trying to feel like.

However, certain drugs can help you get to a place spiritually that may be difficult for you to arrive at without them. If you use them for that purpose and set intentions for your journey, they can be a helpful tool you can use to get to that place without them one day. If used properly, under proper supervision, these medicines can help to raise your overall vibrations. Disclaimer: This is my opinion and not medical advice. Not everything works the same for everyone and you are responsible for your body and what you choose to put in it.

Even though I'm a fan of tequila and fine dry rose' wine (in moderation most of the time), I'm super obsessed with really fun, delicious, high-vibrational non-alcoholic drinks.

Here's my favorite:

The High as Hell Elixir

(Makes one 16 ounce drink)

Ingredients:

Brewed, iced hibiscus, yerba mate, or green tea

Coconut water and/ or kombucha

Pineapple juice

Ice

Lime garnish

Directions:

Fill pint glass with ice.

Fill halfway with tea.

Pour in coconut water, kombucha, or a combo of the two, leaving one inch at the top.

Fill rest with pineapple juice.

Stir.

Garnish with lime.

Drink.

Feel high.

Wake up the next day feeling fabulous!

Here's another favorite:

Sparkly Basil Lemonade

(Makes approximately 4 servings)

Ingredients:

Beyonce's Lemonade album playing in the background

4 cups fresh basil leaves, plus 6 sprigs for garnish

3/4 cup sugar (fairtrade if possible)

1 cup fresh squeezed lemon juice (you'll need about 6 lemons)

Directions:

Place basil leaves, sugar, and 2 cups of water in a saucepan and bring to a boil.

Stir until the sugar is dissolved.

Simmer for 5 minutes and instead of stirring, dance!

Strain by pressing on the basil to get the liquid out.

Let it cool and dance some more.

Pour 2 cups of the magical basil syrup you just made into a large pitcher.

Stir in the lemon juice and add 4 cups of water.

Put it in the fridge until it's super chillaxed.

Serve over ice.

Garnish with basil sprigs.

5. Listen to good music. Jimi Hendrix said, "Music is a safe kind of high." His statement needs a little tweaking to be completely accurate because songs with lyrics of hate, pain, violence, drama, and fear send messages straight up into your subconscious. If you want to attract love, listen to songs about real, passionate, long-lasting love. If you want peace, listen to music that feels relaxing. If you want to drink too much, crash your car, get cheated on by your boyfriend, and get in a fight, listen to music about that!

These are my favorite tunes to get high to:

Turn on Your Lovelight by Bobby Bland

This Little Light of Mine by Avis Burgeson Christiansen

Good Vibrations by Marky Mark and the Funky Bunch

Hey Jude by The Beatles

Blaze On by Phish

Sunshine by Zach Deputy

This Must Be the Place (Naive Melody) by Talking Heads

One Love by Bob Marley

Budding Trees by Nahko and Medicine for the People

6. Get your home high. Paintings, concert posters, photographs, crystals, statues, rocks, mantras, books, magazine, flowers, plants, the colors on the walls, and even the way your furniture is arranged all create energy. Put attention into keeping your home clean, clutter free and organized.

7. Reduce the amount of crap you watch on TV. Programs nowadays are mostly all about the drama, sex, and violence. You're beaming a laser of negativity directly into your living room and subconscious. To make matters worse, there are commercials that have you thinking you need pills to fix your problems, things to purchase to make you happy, and all types of unhealthy foods to put in your body. If you do want to watch television, there are many educational, hysterical and inspirational shows and movies to choose from. You can also choose to watch a concert.

8. Spend time with happy people. Hang out with people who empower you, have similar morals as you, see how incredible you are, and love the wildest expression of your true self.

9. Be kind. Don't do it for the thank you and don't expect one. Do it for the love.

10. Practice compassion and forgiveness. Just thinking thoughts of forgiveness about someone in your past without taking any action will raise your vibration. Imagine what would happen if you did take action?

11. Express gratitude. When I'm feeling really low and craving a little instant gratification, I stop, drop and express gratitude. Shifting my focus to what I have in my life that I feel grateful for, my vibration instantly and dramatically rises. Each day, take at least thirty seconds for this practice and feel your vibration move on up!

12. Radically and unconditionally love everything. All of the bad events that happen in the world are the result of a lack of love. One of the ways you can raise not only your vibration, but the world's, too, is to do everything from a place of love. Love up your friends. Love up your family. Love up strangers. Love up your enemies. Love up the people who have caused you pain. Love up yourself. You don't have to like everyone and everything, but it's important to love them.

You now have all the tools you need to get high. Live by them.

Smiling's My Favorite (Because it Makes Me Feel High)

"Nothing left to do but smile, smile, smile." ~Robert Hunter

The best way to let your soul shine on even the lowest of low-vibe days is to smile. And yes, even if you don't feel like it. There's a saying, "Fake it til you make it." It's OK to fake it when what you're faking is something that's within you that you want to let out. This isn't just woo-woo information. There is scientific evidence out there that proves it.

Research shows that when your face is making a smile, it triggers something in your brain that makes you actually feel real happiness. If you want to take this happiness thing to the next level, it is recommended by experts that you start each day by waking up with a smile on your face.

If your normal morning face is a sour puss, it's not going to feel natural to remember to smile. I have a Post-It Note on my nightstand that says "Smile you sexy beast," so I have a friendly reminder that makes me giggle a little each morning.

A study in the publication *Psychological Science* shows people who smile often live an average of seven years longer.

Need a little more high vibe inspiration?

Read These Sweet Quotes

I hand-picked my favorite quotes just for you from people who inspire me. All these people are so freakin high-vibe, man.

> "Be your best for the greater good, and rock out wherever you are."
>
> ~Michael Franti

> "The trick was to surrender to the flow."
>
> ~Trey Anastasio

> "Be thankful for what you have; you'll end up having more. If you concentrate on what you don't have, you will never, ever have enough."
>
> ~Oprah Winfrey

"Don't worry. Be Happy."

~Bobby McFerrin

"So many good things come to those who love relentlessly."

~Mihali Savoulidis

"Keep your thoughts positive because your thoughts become your words. Keep your words positive because your words become your behavior. Keep your behavior positive because your behavior becomes your habits. Keep your habits positive because your habits become your values. Keep your values positive because your values become your destiny."

~Mahatma Gandhi

"It's all happening!"

~The Band-Aids from the film *Almost Famous*

"When things go wrong, don't go with them."

~Elvis Presley

"It's difficult to believe in yourself because the idea of self is an artificial construction. You are, in fact, part of the glorious oneness of the Universe. Everything beautiful in the world is within you."

~Russell Brand

"Do not be embarrassed by your failures; learn from them and start again."

~Richard Branson

"Time you enjoy wasting was not wasted."

~John Lennon

"Some people feel the rain. Others just get wet."

~Bob Marley

Suggested Listening:

The Mountain by Trevor Hall
Wasting Time by ALO
Best Feeling Keller Williams
Wouldn't it Be Nice by The Beach Boys
Wonderful (The Way I Feel) My Morning Jacket
Colorado Bluebird Sky The String Cheese Incident

ROCK THE MAGIC!

Make your own High-Vibes Playlist.

Bonus points: Dance to it.

Super bonus point: Invite your friends over to dance with you.

Which of the quotes were your favorite and why?

How can you implement their lessons in your life?

Write down three things you are grateful for right now. Go!

Writing Prompt

What are some low-vibrational activities you are willing to let go of?

Now heartstorm some new high-vibe activities you'll do with your extra time.

Taraleigh Weathers

Reflections

3

MAGIC IS NORMAL

*"Once in awhile you get shown the light
In the strangest of places if you look at it right."*

Scarlet Begonias by the Grateful Dead

mir·a·cle

ˈmirək(ə)l/

noun

1. A surprising and welcome event that is considered Divine.

2. Changing how you think, feel, or deal with something from fear or hatred to love.

3. A term coined by Deadheads, meaning a ticket to a show was given as a gift to someone outside the venue who has no ticket. Usually given randomly by a stranger. Taken from the Grateful Dead song "I Need a Miracle."

"I was walking around the parking lot before the show when this guy came up and miracled me."

You know when you're thinking of a friend and then they call you? Or when you're looking for a parking space and you find one easily right in front? Or when you hear a song in your head and then turn on the radio and it's playing? When things like that happen, I used to say things like, "That's crazy!" and "I can't believe it!"

My languaging was pretty much telling the Universe that I'm shocked that it was capable of that much awesomeness. Nowadays, I say, "Magic is normal and I'm so grateful." What I found was that everything — the good, the bad, and the ugly — are all miracles.

Trey Anastasio, the guitarist for the band Phish, was in a drug and alcohol induced haze swerving down a dark road in Whitehall, New York, on a fateful evening in 2006. Eventually, the police caught wind of his reckless driving and Trey got pulled over and arrested. He was sentenced to some jail time and fourteen months of community service, where he was forced to scrub toilets and clean fairgrounds.

Being a huge fan of Trey and his music, I had been silently rooting for him to get healthy. After witnessing Phish's final lackluster show that took place in Coventry, Vermont, something was obviously very wrong with the guitarist. His normally almost flawless playing was all over the place and he seemed to be checked out from life. When I learned what had happened that night in Whitehall, I wasn't surprised. I felt a deep sadness that someone so magical and talented could have fallen so far off his unicorn.

A couple of years later in 2013, Trey shared at a rally for drug courts on Capitol Hill in Albany, New York: "My life had become a catastrophe. I had no idea how to turn it around. My band had broken up. I had almost lost my family. My whole life had devolved into a disaster. I believe that the police officer who stopped me at 3:00 a.m. that morning saved my life."

"When Phish broke up, I made some comment about how I'm not gonna go around playing 'You Enjoy Myself' [one of Phish's most popular songs] for the rest of my life," Anastasio said to *Rolling Stone*. "And it's so funny, because Fish and Mike and Page [the other members of the band] have been talking to each other a lot lately. It's not that I can't believe that I said that, but it's symbolic of how much I lost my mind or how much I lost my bearings or something. Because at this point in time I would give my left nut to play that song five times in a row every day until I die. I certainly thought about that while I was in jail."

At that same rally for drug courts in Albany, Trey said, "I've been sober for two and a half years. My children are happy. In August, my wife and I will celebrate our fifteenth wedding anniversary. My band is back together with a sold-out tour." His statement received massive amounts of applause.

Miracle! Isn't that so normal? I think so and I'm so grateful!

I've gathered miracle stories from people in my life, along with a couple of my own, to show you just how normal life can be. Miracles happen all the time, I'm so grateful and here's the proof.

Taraleigh's New Orleans Miracle

Jazz Fest in New Orleans, Louisiana is an event every music lover should experience at least once in their lifetime. A city that is already bursting at the seams from epic amounts of magic on a daily basis stretches its party pants five sizes larger during those two weekends in early May. Celebration is the theme and music is the avenue that delivers it.

It's easy to forget that a place that has an outward appearance of being so fun and beautiful can have such a dark side to it. New Orleans has an insane homeless situation. Peering over my world-famous frozen hurricane drink I'm blessed to be able to afford, I started to notice all of the people lying on the sidewalks that clearly didn't have homes, much less able to afford a frivolous beverage like the one I was consuming. Looking around even more, I saw that most of the party people didn't even notice or acknowledge these human beings that were obviously struggling. They were being stepped over and ignored like yesterday's garbage.

Amongst the sea of homeless humans, I spotted a man sitting on the ground with his dog. He saw me too and we locked eyes. Looking away because I felt uncomfortable, I walked briskly in the other direction. Something inside me pushed me to turn around and go back to the man and ask him, "Are you hungry?" Not saying a word, he sadly shook his head yes.

New Orleans has a restaurant on every corner, so I walked into the nearest one and bought a meal for him. As he sat on the ground and devoured what seemed like possibly the only food he'd eaten in days, I joined him on the sidewalk. I asked, "How did you get here?"

Tears immediately poured down his weathered cheeks as he said, "I had a good job as an engineer and was really successful. Had a beautiful family too, but one thing led to another and I made a lot of mistakes. Now I'm here and I don't know how to be anywhere else."

"It happened and you can't change the past. You've made some really bad choices in your life and now you're suffering the consequences. Those mistakes don't have to define who you are anymore. You're a different man than you were then and I believe in your ability to get back onto your feet, one step at a time" I said to him with tears streaming down my face too. I looked him in the eyes and said, "I see you."

He hugged me so hard I lost my breath. I don't know what happened to that man or if he found his way off the streets, but what I do know is the power of human connection. He did just as much for me as I did for him that night. We were each other's miracles.

Marinda's Mama is a Miracle

by Marinda Righter

I've been told my whole life that I'm a miracle (though I believe we all are), and the feelings that come from that sentiment are both heart aching and heartfelt. The same accident that killed my father twenty-nine years ago allowed me to walk away without a scratch on my body. I was almost two. My mother was twenty-seven. From that point on, it was just mum and me.

Having never found a man as sweet and genuine as my father, she never remarried. She lived for me and showed me the ways of tolerance, compassion, and a true love for life. For thirty years our bond deepened as we walked hand in hand down a path of loss, heartbreak, and obstacles. However, we were continuously fueled with unconditional love for one another and a great sense of adventure.

The death of a loved one will change a person, heighten their awareness, and make them experience mental and physical feelings they didn't know existed. I was living in New Orleans in February of 2013 when I received a phone call on the first day of Mardi Gras that my mother had had a massive stroke at the young age of fifty-six.

On that nine-hour trip back to Massachusetts, I thought of all of the challenges my mother and I had overcome and how resilient we both were. We spoke often of miracles and the many connections between us all. These conversations echoed in my mind and I found myself holding onto the hope that she'll come through; that this was just another opportunity for a miracle. I was being faced with my past, present, and future simultaneously; an ineffable feeling I don't think could ever be repeated.

The moment I arrived in that hospital room, I knew that this was not a bump in the road; this was a quake, and breath by breath I moved with the earth-shattering news that, "There was nothing else they could do." My nurturer, my best friend, my traveling companion, my rock, and my biggest cheerleader was going on a journey that I could not accompany her on. But I would soon find out that she had an agenda of her own, and her legacy would move and inspire many to follow.

As I filled out the papers for her organ donation, I felt a sense of comfort knowing that her healthy tissues and organs would be bringing life to someone else. It was my mother's selfless spirit and giving nature that made this process "easier." The representative from the New England Organ Bank then asked me a question that would change my life forever.

"Would you be willing to donate your mother's facial tissue?"

He explained how it was quite rare to find a match, but it was possible. With an open yet broken heart, I said yes.

It was a long ride home from the hospital, though it was only an hour to Cambridge. After barely making it up the stairs, I pulled myself into bed and cried like I've never cried before. No more than five minutes later my house started to fill up with many loving friends of mine, all who had known my mother. Before I knew it, we were twenty strong in a cuddle puddle in the living room.

A couple hours into this love fest, I received a call from the New England Organ Bank informing me that they had a match for my mother's facial tissue, and, with my permission, my mother's beautiful face would provide a higher quality of life to someone who truly needed it. So, it was done. On February 14, 2013, some lucky person was going to be wearing a face I've kissed a million times. In hindsight, my life does seem more and more miraculous as it unfolds, and I truly

believe anything is possible. Two things are for certain: You are born into the unknown, and you die into the unknown. What happens in between is your choice. Some choices are harder than others and harder for some people more than others.

I was blessed with a kind, selfless, natural, empathetic Mama who raised me to care for my fellow human beings as I would myself. She taught me to follow my heart, to listen to my intuition, and, if I was ever in trouble, to ask the Universe for guidance. It has the ability to give me the tools I need to persevere, she frequently told me.

The woman who is the recipient of my mother's face is a living miracle. The pain and trauma Carmen Blandin Tarleton had to endure before and while becoming a facial tissue recipient is astounding, and I encourage you to read her book *Overcome: Burned, Blind, and Blessed*. It is truly a miracle that she survived the brutal attack of her estranged husband with industrial-strength lye that burned over 80 percent of her body.

As I have gotten closer to Carmen over the past year, I have come to realize that she and my mother have a similar insight as to how the Universe works.

They also listen to the same music, have read the same books, and have an appreciation for life that many admire, especially having experienced so many hardships. This new chapter, in which my mother and Carmen are connected without having met one another, is not, I believe, by coincidence. Every moment has something to teach us, if we are willing to listen.

When I first met Carmen, three months after she received my mother's gift, I felt a wave of peace and love wash over me. I told her that I felt elated and comfortable in her presence. The miracle of science has allowed me to see my mother's beautiful face, to touch her freckles, to kiss her skin once again. Carmen's openness to a relationship with me is truly a blessing, and I'm thankful every day that my mother's legacy has paved a way for future facial transplants, Carmen's being only the fifth such procedure done to date at Brigham Hospital.

My mother Carmen and I are survivors, and, as life unfolds, I've come to accept there's a reason why. Instead of feeling alone on this journey, I have taken the opportunity to speak of my experiences in the hope that they will inspire and/or heal others. It brings me great comfort to speak of my mother's beautiful selfless nature and the undeniable responsibility she felt to take care of her fellow human beings, sometimes more than herself. In her memory, I am honored to have shared with you a piece of our story about the miracle that ensued because of the little "♥" on her driver's license.

Ryan Montbleau's Fashion Miracle

by Ryan Montbleau: Singer/Songwriter

My miracle sounds silly at first, but bear with me.

It was a fashion miracle.

Now, I'm no fashion plate, but I guess I've always managed to stay "put together" with whatever I'm wearing, day in and day out. When I find something that works, such as a nice pair of shoes or a good hat or a properly-fitting pair of slacks, I tend to wear that thing over and over and over and over again, until it falls apart. And because of that, the first rip in the knee of a well-worn pair of pants can be like a small tragedy. Ripped jeans make me think of Bon Jovi, and I can't have that. Not for one minute. Time for new pants. It can be almost like losing a pet or something. Really hard to replace.

So we were on tour, and I got that fatal knee-rip in a pair of gray corduroys that had been my faithful friend for a good couple of years. They fit perfectly, and it was a very specific brand in a very specific size in a very specific color that made it all work. I liked them so much that I even searched online to buy the same exact ones. (Searching for clothes online! That was a new one for me...) No dice. Impossible to find. Oh well.

We pulled into Philadelphia for a show, and a few of the guys and I took a train across town to visit our friend Steve Hark in the hospital. Steve's an old Deadhead, and he's been to a zillion shows of all kinds over the years, including so many of ours. He loved to dance to live music. He had a huge white head of hair, a fluffy gray and white beard, big bushy eyebrows, bad teeth, a wiry little frame, and he would often say things like, "I love you, man," with this big genuine and wry smile. And he meant it. You had no choice but to love the guy back. The Hark Man! He was tremendous.

As it turned out, Steve's liver was failing, and we had heard about a recent surgery that was crucial to his future. We'd also heard that the situation was bad, but it was not until we walked into his room at the hospital that we realized: "Oh, man. Steve is dying."

It just hit you like a neon sign when you first laid eyes on him. Steve was dying. He was a little more than half his normal skinny self, cheeks were sunken in, tubes coming in and out all over his body. For some reason his teeth were mostly gone, and there was some kind of reddish food-like mush all over his remaining half-teeth and gums. He made sounds to speak but was hard to understand. After a long, tearful visit and some conversation over the sound of long Jerry solos streaming out of my phone, I hugged Steve there in his bed. I told him that I loved him, and he managed to say, "I know."

Then it was time for us to leave.

While sitting there with the guys, looking at my friend, who was so clearly and so feebly on his way out, something struck me as clear as the light of day. I looked at him and thought, "Kindness is so important." Seeing this wonderful, loving man in such a tragic state, how could you not want to be kind to him? How could you not have been kind to him for his whole life? How could you not be kind to anyone in life? Kindness is so important. We're here for a minute, and then we're gone. Kindness is so important.

I decided to walk the two miles back to the club by myself. I passed a guy in the street dressed up like Michael Jackson, dancing for change. I walked through the courtyard in the middle of Independence Hall, and another man was playing some gorgeous music on a violin in the dusky light, the sounds reverberating up the old walls. I cried a little more. I stopped for a slice of pizza. I walked into a second-hand store. There, in the rack of random men's pants from every brand and every decade and every style, I saw a pair of corduroys. Same exact brand as the ones that had just ripped. Same exact size. Same exact color. They looked like they were brand new. And they cost next to nothing.

I'm wearing them as I write this because that's what I do. I wear them until I can't anymore. Now I don't know exactly what the lesson here is. I wish my miracle was that Steve made a dramatic recovery and is now out on tour, dancing the night away with that same grin and those big bushy eyebrows. But that didn't happen. Steve passed away a few days after we saw him. There was no big miracle. But there was this one very, very small and seemingly silly one. A fashion miracle, if you will. And that may sound trite, but life is full of little miracles. In fact, I believe they're everywhere around us, if we can only open ourselves up to them and see them. In that sense, it seems that our job is to make ourselves more aware. And, in my limited experience, something happens to the energy around you when someone you know passes away. Your attention and your awareness heighten. Through all that pain and suffering and passing, you gain some true life wisdom. You become conscious of the rising and passing all around us.

And funny things can happen in that space.

Thanks for the pants, Steve. These things are sweet. I love you, man.

Stephen Kiernan's Sister's Hair Miracle

by Stephen Kiernan: Author of *The Baker's Secret*

A few years ago my younger sister was diagnosed with breast cancer. It was scary for lots of legitimate reasons: She was single parent to five kids, their dad was not in any condition to step in and help, and our mom had died of breast cancer at a relatively young age.

Soon after the diagnosis, Amy had a scan that showed one tumor in the shape of a fork prong. By the time she had surgery, a few weeks later, her breast contained five tumors, all large. Afterward, she faced chemotherapy and a long bout of radiation treatment. These powerful poison-medicines worked, and she is now five years post-diagnosis, which is the timeline doctors use to say she is cancer-free. I tell you that outcome now not to give away the story's ending, but to show that her story was not about illness. It was about life.

Amy had been through two of her chemo treatments when she looked down at the shower drain one morning and saw that it had a toupee's worth of her long hair. She had always been a chesty blonde, and proud of it, but now these feminine powers were all being cut away or falling out of her. She decided not to wait till the chemo had made her bald. Instead Amy called the woman who had cut her hair for years, and made an appointment to have her head shaved.

The woman must have had experience with these situations; she told Amy to come on Friday, after regular business hours. When Amy arrived, there were candles lit, bottles of wine opened, and some of her closest female friends were there. They toasted the loss of her hair, and the hope that it would one day return.

Amy went home that night and her oldest son Chris took one look at her bare head and went upstairs without a word. She thought he must be upset and scared to see his mother looking this way. But when he came back down a few minutes later, Chris had shaved his head. At that, her twins, Peter and Michael, went upstairs and took their turn shaving.

That Friday, Peter and Michael's JV high school football team had a game. Amy had been undecided about whether to go, because she was embarrassed by her lack of hair. But after her sons had been so brave and supportive, she knew she could handle it. She wrapped her head in a fancy scarf, put a hat on top, and sat in the bleachers with the other moms and dads while their 15-year-olds played their hearts out.

At the end of the game, after the players had shaken hands and done their final cheer, the team came over to the sidelines. They faced the bleachers. One by one the boys removed their helmets. Every single one of them was bald. The entire team had shaved its head.

That was the moment Amy stopped being afraid. That was the instant she knew that love was stronger than disease. A bunch of teenage jocks gave her all the faith she needed.

Finding Light in the Darkest of Places: Taraleigh's Story

"Let's let it fly and see what happens," I said to my husband Dan. Flash forward to a year later and my period was a day late. Shaking with anticipation of the unknown and the reality that our lives may be about to change forever, I grabbed a pregnancy test. I had to pee pretty badly when I first picked it up, but after realizing the test would determine the direction of the rest of my life with just my urine stream, I suddenly became pee shy. I gathered up all the strength I could muster and accomplished the task I was setting out to do. My mind went to all kinds of crazy scenarios while impatiently waiting for the results.

"Ummmmmm. Dan. We have a situation!!!" I exclaimed, not able to move off the toilet.

Overwhelmed with excitement, we told our close friends and family the great news right away. Everyone was over the moon excited for us. "Don't tell anyone until you've reached three months because you never know what can happen" we were told by many.

"When do we ever really know what's going to happen?" I thought. I don't know what's going to happen in the next five minutes, let alone nine months from now, but we did keep the news mostly in the family because I guess that's what you're supposed to do.

At nine weeks, we had our first midwife appointment. At that stage of development, a baby looks more like a shark than like a baby, so Dan and I were looking forward to seeing the shark that we loved already for the first time. Probing my insides with a magic wand that allowed us to see what was happening inside my womb, the midwife seemed to catch a glimpse of something that made her easy going, relaxed demeanor shift almost immediately to extreme nervousness. Scurrying out of the room without saying a word, she left my husband and I in a panic. She came back to take another look and explained that the yolk sack was trying to split into two, creating identical twins, but had stopped developing.

My husband and I drove home in silence. In a haze of disbelief, we walked into our bedroom and slept for hours from being emotionally exhausted. Truth be told, I was also avoiding reality and my hope was that if I slept, maybe when I woke up, I would be pleasantly surprised that the whole ordeal was just a dream. I woke up in the middle of the night and made a big mistake.

I went online to research miscarriage.

I found all these blogs with titles like, "This is what to never say to a person who just had a miscarriage." I read things like this:

Don't say, "Things always happen for a reason. It will happen when the time is right."

Don't say, "You are really lucky you weren't that far along."

Most of the things you aren't supposed to say are the things I was thinking to myself that brought me comfort. My mind racing, I thought things like, maybe things don't happen for a reason. Then what the heck is going on? I lost it and cried myself to sleep.

Doing research is OK because it is important to learn all you can about whatever it is you're going through, but know this: No book, blog, or article knows how you're feeling right now or what your next step should be.

The next day I took time to really process what had happened and to grieve the loss of the lives of our babies that never manifested. On top of that, I had to grieve the loss of the hopes and dreams I envisioned for my family that went away when the babies did. I let myself feel all the feels in every moment, even though it was the complete opposite of a rainbows and unicorns situation.

I needed support and most people wanted to help, but in situations like this, they often just don't know how. I reached out to friends and family individually and let them know what happened and how they could best support me.

When I stepped out of the darkness, I shared my story with anyone who was willing to listen. Something I didn't expect happened. Most people either had a story of their own or knew someone else who had gone through a similar thing.

Hearing my loved ones' stories didn't make what happened to me less sad and it didn't invalidate my feelings of loss. What it did do was help me see that I'm not alone in this and that, unfortunately, so many others can relate to that kind of loss. I eventually moved through the pain and was able to to see the lessons I learned from the experience.

Even though that year was a painful one, it was also beautiful. Because of my miscarriage, I was forced to practice surrendering into the unknown at a level I didn't know was possible. Just when I thought I had fully surrendered, I was challenged to surrender a little more. The entire experience taught me to trust in the Divine, let people see the real me that isn't always smiling, and to ask for support and help when I need it.

Joel Cummins' Fifth Year of College Was a Musical Miracle

by Joel Cummins: Keyboardist for Umphrey's McGee

I had a choice. I could graduate from the University of Notre Dame with a theology degree or finish my nearly complete music theory degree and stay for a fifth year. As my college years progressed, I had an increasing hunch that I would be happiest in a music-related field. Then I started dating a girl who would still be in school for what would be my fifth year of studies. This made the decision easier. Back to school won as the reasons to stay began to add up.

In November of '97, drummer Mike Mirro and I (of the popular ND band Stomper Bob) were invited to dinner with two guys: Brendan Bayliss and Ryan Stasik. We had shared a few impromptu jam sessions in recent months, many of them late-night jams after running into each other at parties or bars. But there was a spark in the music we made together, the feeling that we could create something bigger. That day, over burritos at the Mishawaka Brewing Company in Indiana, they made a life-changing proposal to us: Do you want to try to create music for a living? Wouldn't that be more rewarding than sitting behind a desk for the next twenty-five years? They said, "Simple. We'll leave our current band if you leave yours." To most, making the decision to join a band full time out of college would seem completely counterintuitive.

Wasn't I staying in school to finish a degree so I could land a job somewhere?

Sometimes you need to follow your heart. Within twenty-four hours, Mike and I arrived on Brendan's doorstep to tell him not only were we in, but we had already left our old band. Two months and hours upon hours of rehearsal later, the band played its first show, and the girl I was dating told me that I'd made a big mistake by leaving Stomper Bob. Sensing her unwillingness to embrace my new life vision, that was the end of the road for the girlfriend. Yet she had been one of the main reasons I was there to start a new band in the first place.

Ironically, sticking around to get my degree had led me down a road where I would never have to use my college education to obtain a job. But am I using my music theory degree every day? Absolutely. Most importantly, though, I made a couple of unrelated decisions that put me in the right place at the right time in my life, as I chose what was right for me at that moment. Without the decision to come back for a fifth year at the University of Notre Dame, there would be no Umphrey's McGee.

Olivia's New Friend

by Olivia Kaufman: RN, BSN, OCN

I was walking my dog Talulah down the street after a tear-filled vet visit. The kind you never wanna have, where you talk candidly about senior dogs and how you want their final months to play out. I don't just have a senior dog. I have a senior dog with an awful illness and we're struggling on all fronts to manage it. Feeling down, but oh so grateful for my wonderful vet and the staff, I slowly dragged myself and Lulu out the door for a little walk before the sun went down.

I like giving Lu opportunities to experience new smells, so it felt right to walk her there. Blocks later, I was approaching the vet clinic again, when a man stepped from his car, wanting to say hello to Lulu. I now know he's a 73-year-old man named Kevin. He told me about how he lost his dog at age 17, and how he coped with it, while also comforting me as I held back tears talking about how sick my own dog is. He hugged me tight and told me I was doing my best.

More dog pats and moments later, the conversation evolved. We talked about the healthcare system, how he's been receiving care for HIV since he was infected in 1984, and that much of his care has been covered. He mentioned his partner who he said was buried back east, who I think may have died from AIDS. He wondered out loud why he was special and survived, when so many in his community hadn't. He wondered why he apparently was lucky and deserving and they were not.

We talked about my brother dying, and how grief is a suitcase that must go with you every single place you do, and that you can never truly unpack it. We talked about the viruses in general, socialized medicine, dogs again. We talked about where we grew up, that in the deep south his neighbors threatened him and taunted him after his partner's sister outed him as a gay man. I told him about the type of education I got, and how I wish everyone had that same opportunity; one where they'd be free to be themselves, and would be curious and open to learn about others and what makes them unique and different.

We talked about podcasts and NPR. He was recently interviewed about his long-term survival as an HIV+ man. And we talked politics. Not just politics now, but over the course of history. We talked about wars and the Holocaust, and then about Trump. We politically align similarly, and are both aghast at the Trump presidency. But again, he offered me comfort.

He said he'd been like me before - full of grief, anxiety, sadness, fear, and anger about the political climate. He respected my process, but also told me about how he now instead tries to act with compassion rather than reflexive anger. He kept saying how the only way to reach people is to ask questions, to be patient, and to try to understand why they think the way they do, and that most people aren't evil, but misinformed and miseducated. He said that it will rip us apart to approach the bigoted and hateful actions of others with more hate.

I've known this for a long time, but feeling hatred back towards these alt-right people is just a knee jerk reaction that I just can't seem to escape. Even though every cell in my body tells me to smash these ideologies with my (in my own opinion) superior knowledge and insights, it's not the way to do it. Kevin was trying to teach me patience and compassion, and to seek it out when it's the hardest. He was teaching me that love will always win, and that we can't confront hate with hate. It felt good to have another human voice this to me.

He said that as long as America has been a thing, we've been in similarly miserable situations. Past presidents have done terrible things, and their supporting governments have let them. He said that it's a matter of time before we exit this darkness towards something bigger and better, and that music and art will become even more beautiful once this heavy and suffocating government loses their power, and that the thinkers and the feelers and the compassionate souls will rise to the top and lead, knowing what's truly at stake.

I spent 50 minutes with Kevin, just outside of his home. The sky went from gray to black while we stood there. We were rained on 3 times. Talulah slept through everything. Kevin gave me hope. He got me to remember that in order to take care of my tender heart, I have to practice compassion everywhere; to me, to those whom I love, and those for whom I feel hatred. I don't have to like them, and I don't have to respect their values. But it definitely helps to approach with some level of compassion, wanting to learn why others think the way they do, and then offer them a different way of thinking without belittling them. No racist or bigot or homophobe, or anti-semite, or Islamophobe or alt-right neo-Nazi member will change when confronted with hatred. It's the language they already speak, so it's nothing new to them.

I've felt so burdened by my anger that it's almost become impossible for me to feel any other way. Kevin helped me look at my anger through a new lens that won't be so exhausting. I will always stay some level of angry, because that's how I get shit done. But letting it consume me and swallow me whole is only hurting me. Gentle reminders to practice compassion and patience is far more beneficial.

Lastly, we finished with another hug, both of us freezing, kind of damp, and definitely underdressed. I told him I'm glad he's here, that he's made it 34 years with an illness that took so many of his friends. I told him the world needed him. I didn't say it directly, but I wanted to tell him that I needed him. But I didn't have to. I think he knew that.

Thank you, Kevin. <3

Jessica Burbridge's Full-Circle Miracle

by Jessica Burbridge: Gorilla Conservationist, Photographer, and Mama

Last week, my friend and fellow gorilla conservationist Emmanuel de Merode, the Virunga National Park Chief Park Warden, was attacked by unidentified rebel gunmen in DRC. Emmanuel was driving from the capital city of Goma to the park headquarters when his truck came under fire from motorcycle-riding assailants armed with AK-47s.

I'm sad to admit that it really didn't come as a big surprise. We've all been waiting for something like this to happen for a long time. A country that has long been rife with violence and exploitation, the Democratic Republic of Congo is dangerous for me and all of my fellow gorilla conservationists. But Emmanuel has a price on his head.

A Belgian prince and anthropologist, Emmanuel has worked tirelessly, in extremely dangerous and difficult conditions, to protect Africa's oldest national park from poaching and international corporations eager to exploit the park's wealth of natural resources. He became the chief park warden in 2007, replacing Honore Mashagiro, who was notoriously linked to the Rugendo group massacre of silverback Senkwekwe, five female gorillas and an infant that year. Over the last six years as park warden, Emmanuel had endured many hardships, struggling to keep his team of 680 rangers safe and well equipped, often having to negotiate with rebel warlords in order to continue to protect the park's critically endangered mountain gorilla population. Over the last ten years alone, the park has lost over 140 rangers in the line of duty.

Emmanuel is one of my greatest heroes. Seven years ago, I was in my early twenties, and I'd just finished my BFA from the Savannah College of Art and Design. Thoroughly befuddled by my burgeoning career, I was unsure of which road to take or how to break into the conservation world I so desperately wanted to be a part of. One evening, while lying in the bathtub, I was reading a National Geographic magazine. This particular issue highlighted the 2007 mountain gorilla family massacre in DRC and discussed Emmanuel's heroic efforts to help the park recover from years of exploitation and deceitful leadership. Before reading this article at this time in my life, the DRC and its majestic mountain gorillas were a dream to me; it was simply a foreign, magical place in my young twenty-something-year-old mind.

I'll never forget the impact that article had on me. Finishing the last paragraph, I launched out of the tub, toweled off, plopped down in front of the computer, and started reaching out to every ape sanctuary in Africa to offer my services as a photographer.

While I received a plethora of "No, thank yous" and ran up against countless brick walls, one opportunity panned out, and soon I was on a plane to Uganda to begin my life's work in Africa.

As things tend to go with one's career, one thing led to another, and before long I was working for the Dian Fossey Gorilla Fund International in Rwanda as their field communications officer. One hot afternoon in October, I found myself sitting as copilot with my hero, Emmanuel de Merode, in his small Cessna airplane, an infant orphaned Grauer's gorilla named Shamavu sitting on the veterinarian's lap behind us.

We were taking this infant to his new home, at the GRACE (Gorilla Rehabilitation and Conservation Education Center) sanctuary in DRC where he would join other youngsters

who had also been orphaned by poachers. Here I was, sitting next to Emmanuel de Merode, flying over Virunga National Park, sipping coffee and discussing the state of conservation in DRC. I lost count of the number of times I wanted to pinch myself to see if it was all just a dream.

It's been two years since I met Emmanuel for the first time. I am now the Director of Marketing and Communications for the Gorilla Doctors, an organization dedicated to saving eastern lowland gorillas, also known as Grauer's gorillas, through hands-on veterinary care in the wild.

Emmanuel is widely revered among the Gorilla Doctors family, as well as all of our partners. Everyone knows the enormous sacrifices he makes to save Virunga National Park. Indeed, his existence is the symbolic shield of the park in many minds.

Fortunately, the Congolese army was swift to take action when Emmanuel was attacked on the Rumangabo road last week. Armored trucks were dispatched to rescue the park warden, and he underwent emergency surgery to remove four bullets from his abdomen by UN doctors in a Goma hospital. All four bullets missed his spinal chord and major organs. He has a long recovery ahead, but he will survive. Having almost paid the final price for conservation, he is the ultimate protector of African wildlife, and will always be a true hero and inspiration to me.

Taraleigh's Delayed Flight Miracle

When I first found out my flight was delayed, my initial reaction was to be mad about it. I sometimes find myself saying that I don't have enough time in the day, and here I was just granted extra time, where I had nothing to do and nowhere to be. I closed my eyes and thanked the Universe and said to myself, "I am open to the magic and miracles that are happening right now all around me."

I was looking for a place to sit when I spotted a wild-looking man with a white beard, a fishing hat on his head, and a big gap between his two front teeth. He looked like a very interesting fellow, so I sat down next to him. After saying hello and introducing myself, I found out that he was from Louisiana and his name was Marcel. I asked him why he was traveling and he shared with me that he's going to Vermont to say goodbye to his younger brother, who was in hospice.

The reason I was traveling was because I was doing a site visit for a retreat in Boone, NC. I was a little bummed because the retreat center was not the right fit for what I was looking to do, but while I was there I met a woman named Lorna Bell. She wrote a book called *Happy Endings,* which was a collection of uplifting end of life stories. She gave me a copy of the book, so I pulled it out of my bag and asked Marcel if he would like to read some stories from the book.

Marcel took the book from me and started to read. A couple of moments later he started to weep. He looked me in the eyes and said with a strong southern drawl, "Wow. It's so clear that we're all one and never alone. I'm going to share this story with my brother. It will bring him and me comfort. Thank you."

A man in a wheelchair with an injured ankle named Alex overheard us talking and joined in on the conversation. Alex is a busy journalist who travels a lot. His dad recently fell ill, and because of his busy schedule, he never had the time to see him.

When I asked him about how he felt about his injury, he shared how mad and frustrated he was about it. He was forced to slow down and he had to pass on a bunch of work assignments because of it. Suddenly a huge smile took over his face. I asked him what was up and he said, "Actually, I'm really grateful for my injury. Because of it, I ended up having some extra time and I went to Brazil to be there for my dad, and it was beautiful and healing for the both of us. If I hadn't hurt myself I would have probably not made the trip."

I said, "That Universe sure is a bitch if you don't listen and do things that aren't in alignment for the greatest good." We all cracked up at my woo-woo/sassy languaging.

The three of us talked for over an hour about the Universe, how to tune into it, why listening to signs helps you to avoid Universal bitch slaps, and how we're all in this thing called life together. It was a true miracle that happened because we were granted some free time by a delayed flight.

Morella Housing Miracle

by Morella DeVost: Counselor and Hypnotherapist

Around springtime last year, I decided I needed to move. My living arrangements were no longer working for me, and I knew I needed to find a new place to live by the end of that summer. I found a great house. It was a newly renovated five-bedroom, two-bathroom house, with a great open floor design and awesome kitchen, and it was in the perfect location.

It was a dream! I had great roommates in the works, and it all seemed so perfect and meant to be, because it was unfolding so easily.

My current roommate and I were ready to sign the lease when, on the first Friday in August, I got a call from my roommate, telling me that he was having second thoughts and wasn't sure he could move forward.

Before we had hung up the phone, he had fully gone from not being sure to completely backing out.

I was livid. He was the one who had come up with the idea to begin with!

We've been talking about it for two months, and now that we're down to the wire, you're telling me that you're out?! I wasted all this time these past two months looking at places. I was pissed! I was mortified to let the landlord know that we were backing out.

Then, all of a sudden, like a lightning strike that woke me up, I thought, "What if I choose to see this as the best possible news I could have gotten today? What is possible now?" A few minutes after I had asked myself the question, my dad asked if I wanted to join him at the neighbor's place for cocktails. Honestly, I was still mad and feeling like I should spend as much time as possible looking for apartments to visit. However, I figured, "What the hey! It's not like those apartments are going to go anywhere." So I went with him.

At the neighbor's gathering, one of them asked me, "Did you find a place?" I rolled my eyes and told her the story, that I had a place but it had just fallen through. She said, "Well, I think so-and- so is moving out at the end of the month!" Sure enough, a neighbor, two doors down from my parents, was moving out at the end of the month. And get this: She hadn't told the landlord yet, so by the time I called him on Monday, he had only just learned that she was leaving. And when we spoke, he said, "Everyone in the neighborhood likes you, and you sound like a lovely person, so I'm not even going to list it. It's yours!"

I am convinced that my decision to ask, "What if this is the best possible news I could have gotten?" transformed the field of possibilities in front of me. At the very least it helped me open my eyes and peel myself away from the computer to go visit with the neighbors.

My place? When I pull my shades in the morning, I gaze out on the lake and the Adirondacks, and I feel so blessed every single time. And I'm two doors down from my parents. Some people might not be thrilled by that, but I absolutely love it!

And what about my roommate? Well, it turned out that he was listening to his intuition beautifully. He had to move out of the state about six weeks after we would have moved into our communal house!

So my invitation to everyone is this: In the face of what seems like really bad news or an unhappy turn of events, ask the Universe, "What if this is the best thing that could be happening right now? What is possible now?" And watch the miracles unfold.

Stephanie's Girl-Power Miracle

by Stephanie Spivak: Massage Therapist

I lead this girls group called "Girls on Fire" at my Boys & Girls Club, which is an anti-bullying group that builds self-esteem and friendship for nine to twelve-year-old girls. Now, my girls can be pretty spunky and sometimes downright mean to each other, but last night there was magic. I threw a Valentine's party for them where we made snacks and bracelets. As the girls were snacking, I asked them to go around the circle and share one thing they love about themselves and the girl sitting to their right. Normally, there would be girls saying they don't like the person next to them or just refusing to participate.

Instead, they took turns sharing incredible, beautiful things about their neighbor (even though some are enemies). Then they wanted to go around again and say something they love about the person to their left. And then again about everyone else in the room. They spent about forty-five minutes just talking about how much they really love each other. The girls were glowing and were all so kind to each other as the night ended. It was just such a cool and proud moment, and we called it the Lovefest.

Erin's Adoption Miracle

by Erin Campos

The year was 2003 and I had been anticipating the eighteenth birthday of my son, whom I had last seen two days after his birth. I decided to contact the organization that handled the adoption to make sure that all of my information was up to date in case my son wanted to find me.

The person I spoke to looked up the records and let me know that they had an envelope in my file from my son's adoptive parents with notes, pictures, and artwork. The woman asked me if I wanted it sent to me, and of course I said yes.

I anxiously awaited the envelope that contained the only information about my son that I could find, other than his birth information and the pictures of him when he was only days old.

On Saturday morning, my daughter, who was almost fifteen years old at the time, went to the post office with me. We were so excited and unsure of what we would find. Once we received the envelope, we tore it open immediately. As we were flipping through the photos my daughter spotted a class picture from a year ago. She looked at me with wide eyes and exclaimed, "Mom. This boy goes to my school!"

I couldn't believe it, so I tried to convince her that he looked like a lot of other teenage boys and that there was no way he goes to her school. We were under the impression that the adoptive family lived in New York or New Jersey. My daughter kept on insisting and made me drive home so she could get her school's yearbook to see if it was indeed her brother.

She flipped through the pages and with tears in her eyes pointed to a picture. It was the exact photograph we had just pulled out of the envelope!

The panic set in. I called the adoption agency immediately and left a frantic message to please call me back right away. I was afraid leave my house for fear that I wouldn't be able to contain myself if we happened to bump into each other.

The agency called me back and they let me know that my son's family were open to arranging a meeting. Patrick, my son, along with his mom, Patti, and dad, Rick, myself, and my daughter all met a couple of days later at a local counselor's office. It was love at first sight! Since that day, we have merged our two families together. I'm so grateful to Patrick's parents for doing such an amazing job raising my son.

Life is Happening For You and Not to You

I gathered these particular stories for you to show that all the things in your life, the good, the bad and the ugly are all happening for you. As you can see, oftentimes when you're in the thick of the experience, it's almost impossible to see how something so awful could possibly have a greater purpose or be happening for your benefit. Almost being the key word. My challenge for you is when you are 'in it,' take a step back from the situation and ask yourself, "What if this is happening for me and for the greatest good of the world. What would that mean?"

Suggested Listening:

Do You Believe in Magic by The Lovin Spoonful
I Need a Miracle by The Grateful Dead
Miracles by Coldplay
Wait for the Moment by Vulfpeck
When It Rains It Pours by Twiddle
Every Little Thing She Does is Magic by The Police
Miracle of Miracles from Fiddler on the Roof

ROCK THE MAGIC!

Make a Miracle Jar

Directions: Find a large mason jar or box that you can set near your bed, a stack of notecards or post it notes, pretty markers, crayons or pens. Every night before going to bed, write down the 'normal' miracles (big and small) that you experienced that day.

Writing Prompt

We've all experienced miracles in our lives, even if we didn't recognize it at the time. Journal about a miracle you remember experiencing.

Reflections:

4

ACHIEVE SELF-CARE SUPERHERO STATUS

"You gotta fight for your right to party."

(You Gotta) Fight For Your Right by the Beastie Boys

It's a bird.

It's a plane.
It's someone practicing yoga?

The planet we call home is in dire straits right now and we need your help. The people of planet Earth are counting on you. What you must do next is vital. No questions asked. Make an appointment to get a massage, go for a walk, purchase a ticket to a live music show, listen to your favorite song, and/or hug a baby STAT. Let's do this!

One morning I was having a heart to heart with the Universe because I was concerned about how it was doing. I asked if it was making time for self-care since it must be so busy with day-to-day life. You know, like making sure the earth continues to spin and other important stuff like that. I received an answer to my question that was so simple and so clear.

Making time to practice self-care for myself, I was, in turn, giving self-care to the world.

The more loving actions toward myself I took, the more energy I had to love up everyone in my life and beyond. The better I took care of my body, the less miracles would have to be performed to keep me healthy. And that, in turn, makes the Universe (and all of us since we're one and the same) feel more awesome too. I then heard, "Please share this information with the world." I shouted, "Hell yes!! I can surely do that."

Self-Care Superhero-ness starts the moment you wake up. Leave your hypothetical cape on your nightstand, so you can pretend to put it on first thing in the morning.

Sometimes I forget it's there.

I'm lying on a beach in paradise while a strikingly handsome man is fanning me and feeding me grapes and green juice. He asks me what I'm doing just lying there doing nothing, when I realize that it's a dream. I pop open one eye with as little effort as possible to catch a glimpse of the time. My alarm is about to go off and I'm pissed about it. I set it to the latest possible moment for me to be able to barely get myself together and out the door. Even though I know it's coming, my alarm scares the sparkles out of me and I leap out of bed with such force that I slam my entire body against the wall. "Was that wall always so close to the bed?" I wondered angrily.

"Jeez. It's going to be one of those days," I say to myself.

Guess what happens? My bad attitude perpetuates the situation. I'm so frazzled because of the lack of time I allowed myself to get ready that I don't have even a spare second to put on an outfit I feel good in, eat breakfast, meditate or write in my journal. Since I'm so off my game already, all hope is lost for the rest of the day. I end up skipping my yoga class, eating lunch at my desk, binging on donuts and I even yelled at the poor cashier at the coffee shop.

I lived a life where I was exhausted, angry, and always sick for years. Don't be like me. Make some changes now.

The first change I made was to start my day with a ten minute mini-festival full of stuff I loved to do. I thought that it sounded great in theory, but I believed that I just didn't have the time, not even ten minutes! Much to my surprise, I found out that when I made my festival time a priority, I somehow always had the time to do it. I had to slay some time vampires like screen time before bed and hitting the snooze button in the morning to make it happen. Surprisingly, I found my not-a-morning-person-self setting my alarm clock ten minutes earlier because my morning mini-festivals were really that beneficial to my well-being.

Your next question is probably, "How could festival-ing in the morning possibly help me be a more productive member of society?" Just a couple of minutes each morning has the potential to ignite the fire within, giving you energy that'll stay with you throughout your day. First thing festival-ing is a very serious part of being a superhero because feeling good is contagious. That's the kind of disease you want to spread out to every man, woman, child and animal you come in contact with.

You can do whatever you want at your morning mini-festival. I created a pre-made list of self-care activities that I named my Life is a Festival Menu. This menu is comprised of at least twenty-five things that nourish my soul like real life festivals do. I not only use mine in the morning, but anytime I desire a little self-care boost. Activities that take a minute, activities that take hours, and everything in between are all on my list. Make your menu chock full of exciting possibilities that jazz you up.

After you've completed your list, make several copies of it, so you have one everywhere you go. Post one next to your bed for your morning mini-festival, in your kitchen, in your car, in your office, on your cell phone, and/or on your computer. It's not just for when you feel bored, sad, or lethargic; it's to be used everyday to keep that festival feeling alive within you.

Here's a sample of my Life is a Festival Menu:

1. Have a dance party.

2. Get dressed in my favorite festival clothes.

3. Handwrite a letter to a friend.

4. Call a someone you met at a festival.

5. Take a bubble bath.

6. Get a massage.

7. Go for a stroll outside.

8. Hula hoop in the yard.

9. Go window shopping.

10. Make a handmade gift.

11. Paint.

12. Go for a run.

13. Practice yoga postures.

14. Make up fantasy festival line-ups and set lists.

15. Braid my hair.

16. Look at my photographs from festivals.

17. Color.

18. Make a fun playlist.

19. Experiment with crazy make-up, temporary tattoos, and glitter.

20. Meditate.

21. Stretch.

22. Go for a hike.

23. Sing a song.

24. Do a card reading for myself.

25. Write in my journal.

Sneak in Your Self-Care

On top of rocking your menu, I bet there are super sneaky ways you can get a little self-care in. Here are some examples: When you're at a stoplight, take a moment to focus on your breath and be present. If you are stuck in traffic, put on a song and rock out. Stretch at your desk while you're at work. Meditate in the shower. Think of three things you're grateful for when you're brushing your teeth. Listen to music that inspires you or guided meditations when making meals.

Have a Hot Love Affair with Yourself!

Driving frantically from fast-food restaurant to fast-food restaurant, raiding their dollar menus and stuffing everything fried and full of sugar I could find into my mouth searching for a satisfaction that never came, I found myself only filled with grease and guilt. When I returned to my cluttered and dirty home where my boyfriend had basically moved himself in, I tiptoed on eggshells. I never knew what emotional state my boyfriend was going to be in when I arrived. He could shower me with gifts and love or explode in a tirade of screaming, breaking my possessions and hitting me. I accepted this as my norm because it's what I thought I deserved.

I had given up. As my Grammy Helen would say, "I was schlepping around looking like a schmatta."

I was a really good actress. I presented myself to the world as someone who unconditionally loved herself, when the truth was I loathed who I had become. I treated myself in ways I wouldn't treat my worst enemy.

I was craving a shift of epic proportions and I knew the only one who could get me out of my funk was me. Life was passing me by, and I didn't want to miss another minute of it being a nincompoop. Did I have the inner strength to do it? I didn't know, but I thought, what's the harm in trying?

Deciding that I would act as though I loved myself right now, even if sometimes I felt like I was a big faker, was the plan. I started out right away by doing things people who loved themselves would do. Not after I had the perfect boyfriend or lived in the perfect place or had the perfect body. Not after anything, but right away! Slowly but surely my plan worked and I started to actually love myself for real.

All those things in my life that I couldn't figure out how to let go of, like my abusive boyfriend, the fast food addiction and the copious amount of clutter? They naturally crowded out and got replaced with all things awesome.

The Secret to Living a Long Life
Hint: Experiencing Live Music is the Fountain of Youth

Living a long life that's thriving, healthy, joyful, passionate, ripe with sweet experiences, surrounded by awesome people, and full of delicious, clean foods is the dream. You only live once (or maybe more depending on your belief system), but, either way, the important thing to remember is if you are going to live to be a vibrant elderly person who rages shows well into their 90's and beyond, you've gotta start making good choices today.

Follow these tips and you are guaranteed to live a long, healthy, and happy life (unless after you read this, you step outside and get hit by a truck):

Make moving fun. Your body was built for action, so every single day you need to move it. It may sound daunting, but what if you made it fun instead? Hate running? Don't run. Despise dancing? Don't dance. It's very hard to stick to something for the long haul if you don't look forward to doing it. It's human nature to stick to activities that bring great pleasure.

Try new things. Is there something out there that you've always wanted to try like curling or playing the drums? Your brain thrives on being challenged to learn new things.

Act like an active person. Walk or bike instead of driving. Park far away from your final destination. Take the stairs. Play with your children. Dance at weddings. Trade your traditional desk for a standing one.

Find your tribe. Make a list of where folks like you hang out. Go to those places and connect with those peeps. Join a club. Go to a meet-up. Make plans to go to a concert. Participate in activities that excite you. If nothing like this exists where you live, create it! Build it, and your people will come.

Surround yourself with shiny happy people. When you hang out with people who are healthy and happy, you will naturally feel healthier and happier too. It's easier to make good choices if your friends are making those choices too.

Build strong family relationships. You have the power to change your family legacy. Holding onto a grudge against a family member? Be the first one to forgive. Don't talk often enough? Be the one to pick up the phone. This includes soul family.

Get it on!! Research shows that tapping that sweet ass on the reg reduces stress, is a great workout, and it leaves you with a beautiful glow. Don't have a partner? Go solo! P.S.A from an old married lady (me): If you're single and mingling, or in an open relationship, please be safe and use protection. Your body is your sacred temple. Don't grant just anyone permission to enter.

I'm about to give you so many good pick up lines because a healthy sex life is good for you. You're welcome in advance.

- A woman doubles her estrogen levels while having sex, which makes her hair shinier and her skin softer.

- Sweating while having sex cleanses the pores, leaving your skin glowing.
- Sex burns calories. You can burn up to two hundred calories per session which is equal to running fifteen minutes on a treadmill.
- It tones your muscles.
- Sex is a natural pain reliever. You can screw your aches away.
- Kissing stimulates saliva production, which naturally cleanses your teeth making you less susceptible to cavities and gum disease.
- Sex is good for circulation as it gets your blood flowing.
- It's awesome for bladder control as sex strengthens your pelvic floor muscles. Pissing your pants is a great way to not get laid.
- Sex is said to improve sleep quality. After an orgasm, you naturally feel sleepy.

Go the F to sleep. Lack of sleep is linked to many health issues. This is why catching your zzz's is essential for your longevity:

- Sleep may reduce your risk of cancer and other diseases.
- Deep sleep is essential to healing the body. Tip: Use a sleep mask to block out all artificial and natural lights in your bedroom to achieve deep sleep.
- Insufficient amounts of sleep will disrupt your natural sleep cycle, making you tired during the day.
- If you don't go to dreamland enough, you are more likely to turn to foods containing sugar and caffeine to give you enough energy to stay awake. The better you sleep, the easier it is to make healthy choices when it comes to your diet.
- When you're sleep deprived, everything starts to hurt. Your head hurts; your back hurts; your skin hurts; your knees hurt.
- People who get enough sleep are able to focus better. They are better friends, better workers, and better partners.

Eat real food. Diets consisting of real, whole foods that are at least 80 percent plants will keep you healthy. Indulging in not-so-healthy foods once in a while won't kill you. While you're at it, slow down and enjoy consuming your food. Interesting fact alert: If you can grow your own garden, that's even better, because research has shown that being responsible for the food you eat can prolong your life.

Don't smoke tobacco cigarettes. Seek support to quit because squashing a smoking habit is extremely hard.

Have faith. Whatever it is you believe in, have faith and trust in something bigger than yourself. Connect daily with the Divine Being, God, Buddha, Allah, Santa Claus, Jerry Garcia, Source, the Universe, or whatever or whoever else you believe in.

Love hard! It's all you need to know. The end.

Suggested Listening:

You Enjoy Myself by Phish
Nightswimming by REM
Follow the Sun by Xavier Rudd
An Invitation by Rising Appalachia
I Love Me by Meghan Trainor
The Greatest Love of All by Whitney Houston
Supernova by the Motet

ROCK THE
MAGIC!

Create your very own Life is a Festival Menu.

1.

2.

3.

4.

5.

6.

7.

8.

9.

10.

11.

12.

13.

14.

15.

16.

17.

18.

19.

20.

21.

22.

23.

24.

25.

Bonus points: Schedule three Life is a Festival Menu items into your week.

Writing Prompts

How can you infuse a little self-care into your daily tasks?

Reflections

5

SLAY THE TIME AND ENERGY VAMPIRES

"I'm on the fence I balance on each shakey board
Tell each side what they want to hear so they won't
get sore
And when heaven rains down and hell seeps up
through the soil
I'll be dancing for the devil and singing for the lord"

Hey Mister by Hayley Jane

I'm well aware that my yoga class is starting fifteen minutes from now, and if I want to avoid rushing to get there, I need to leave this very moment. Yoga is so important for the health of my mind, body and spirit, and when I miss it, I feel the consequences in every aspect of my life.

Instead of getting myself together to arrive to class on time with ease, I make another choice; I plan on taking 'just a minute' to casually peruse through my Facebook feed to see if anything interesting is happening with any of my 5,000 friends. Without my conscious consent, I find myself flying full speed into the social media rabbit hole checking out how my ex-boyfriend's family is doing and scrolling through someone I don't even know in real life's vacation photos from Belize. As this happens and I fall deeper into the abyss and my time to get to yoga class is going swiftly down the drain. I sneak in a quick glimpse at the clock and damn it! Class started five minutes ago.

"I'm so busy! I don't have enough time to go to yoga," I think, lying to myself.

One of the most valuable assets we have in this life is our time and our energy. What's eating away at yours? Let's figure it out and do a cleanse of the biggest culprits.

Some of the most common energy vampires and time vampires are:

- Excessively being on the internet (checking out ex-boyfriends/girlfriends/friends/lovers' profiles on social media, stalking your own social media walls and pages, and/or spending a lot of time on message boards)
- Gossiping
- Avoiding doing something that really needs to get done
- Watching television
- Complaining
- Having an unorganized, cluttered house, office, and/or car

- Taking part in and/or causing dramatic situations
- Doing things you feel like you should be doing out of obligation
- Saying yes too much; never saying no
- Constantly worrying about stuff that's out of your control
- Not getting enough restful sleep

My sweet blood was being sucked by vampires, and I knew I needed to do something about it. My most popular sayings were, "I don't have enough time," "Where did the time go?" and "I'm so tired." Craving more spaciousness in my life, I jotted down every single thing I did for three days.

I was shocked to see how many time and energy vampires had weaseled their way into my life behind my back. So much of my precious time was getting wasted on pointless distractions. Seeing it laid out in front of me, it was so clear as to why I felt so frazzled, tired, pressed for time and drained. Change was going to have to happen if I wanted to slay those vampires for good.

I started with time vampires.

How to Stab the Time Vampires in the Heart with a Stake of Love

Schedule more time than you actually need to accomplish things. Put everything you're up to in your planner, scheduling more than enough time to complete it. Life continues to change and can throw you daily curve balls that take time to resolve. If you've only given yourself the exact amount of time to do each task, you'll feel rushed and often find yourself late. When you're late, you become a time vampire yourself, because you're taking up someone else's valuable time. Not cool bro.

Limit your online time. I have a nasty habit of spending excessive amounts of time on social media. My solution is to remove all social media apps from my phone, schedule limited social media time and set a timer to keep me on track. When I take to the internet mindlessly, I get myself into big trouble. Before logging on, I set an intention for my surfing. If I'm to connect with people or I want to get inspired, I make sure that is what I actually do during my scheduled internet time.

Don't always answer phone calls or emails immediately. Some people expect you to drop whatever you're doing and be at their beck and call. This knee-jerk reaction to feel the need to act right away can make you feel anxious and always on call. The world will not implode if you take a couple of deep breaths, a couple of minutes or even a couple of hours before responding. If you have a call with a person who has a habit of going on and on, set a timer and get off the phone when the timer goes off. Hold on to your boundaries.

Limit the amount of television you watch or kill your TV all together. The thought of not watching television at all seems insane to most people. How much of your time do you spend sitting in front of the tube? Ask yourself, "Is this use of time for my highest good?" Come up with an amount of time that feels good and set a timer for when it's time to turn the TV off, and then actually turn it off.

Clear out and organize your home and car. I used to spend countless hours searching for my keys, my favorite hoodie, the salt, or my unicorn horn. To avoid the constant looking, I put aside some time to clear out excess stuff and set up a system that works for me so I don't have to waste time in the future. Some ideas: Sort thru your clothes, accessories, shoes, knickknacks, kitchen utensils, ticket stubs, books etc., determine which items have fulfilled their destiny with you and donate them, consign them, repurpose them, or host a clothing swap. Install a hook for your keys by the door. Put up a shoe rack up in your closet. Designate a spot for the salt and your unicorn horn. Take one space at a time and get creative. If these tasks are too much for you and your head is spinning at the thought of it, there are professionals you can hire to work with you. It's worth every cent.

When you implement what you've just learned, the time vampires in your life won't know what hit them. Time to slay the energy vampires next.

How to Identify an Energy Vampire

Energy vampires are people who suck the positivity and joy right out of you, leaving you completely drained. They try to come off as the victim in most situations, somehow leaving you feeling like you did something wrong. Truly believing that everyone else is responsible for their circumstances, an energy vampire never takes responsibility for their actions. Complaining about life is the norm. They act as though the world revolves around them.

An unsuspecting happy and kind person is the prime target for an energy vampire. That brand of sweet blood is exactly the kind they fiend for. Before your very eyes, they will unapologetically take them for all they've got before moving toward their next victim.

Here's an example of a classic energy vampire: My friend (we'll call him Brian) had a 'friend' (we'll call him Robert) who only wanted to give him the time of day when he was in trouble. The calls were always desperate and wildly dramatic. Robert delivered his best sob stories when he wanted Brian to bail him out of whatever trouble he got himself into, to pick up the bar tab because he 'forgot' his wallet, or to go to the store and buy him food or else he would starve.

I asked Brian to add up how much money he had spent on Robert in the past year. My jaw hit the ground when Brian, who is not a particularly wealthy man, told me that he had spent upwards of ten thousand dollars.

How much money had Brian spent on himself in the past year? Besides the essentials, he hadn't spent a cent on himself. I asked him why, and he said he didn't have any extra money. And that's when the lightbulb went off.

Brian was putting so much of his time and energy into this so-called friend who was just using him as an ATM, leaving him with an overdrawn account. When Brian wanted to talk about his own problems, Robert told him to not be so needy and shut him down and started talking about himself again.

I asked, "What are you going to do with all the extra time and money you'll have once you're done getting taken advantage of? Are you ready to stop enabling Robert?"

As Brian shook his head yes, it was like ten thousand pounds were lifted off his slumped shoulders. He lit up, standing up straighter than ever, and started sharing all the things he was going to do. Since he takes really good care of his shoes, his current pair had thousands of miles and shows on them. His kicks were way past their prime. Like way past. They were falling apart and barely holding on for dear life. The time had officially come for a shiny new pair. Brian's mother was one of his biggest cheerleaders, so next on his list was to to treat her to dinner at her favorite restaurant. With all the extra cash he was saving, signing up for a retreat in Costa Rica would now be possible.

"How did it feel to give Robert all the handouts, leaving you struggling?" I asked.

Brian replied, "Used, worthless, and terrible."

My next question was, "How do you feel when you think about taking your mother to dinner, finally getting some new kicks and going to that retreat?"

Brian replied, "Excited, energized, scared, and ready."

You go Brian!!!

How to Slay an Energy Vampire by Stabbing Them in the Heart with a Stake of Love

Identify and squash the conversations that suck your energy immediately.

Decline any invitations you receive to join the pity party.

Don't listen to, contribute to, or pass on gossip.

Stop enabling bad behavior.

Don't waste energy taking things personally, no matter how personal it feels. It's just stuff getting projected onto you. If necessary, confront the energy vampire in a loving way, without the expectation that they will respond lovingly back.

Two questions I have had to ask myself when holding on to an energy vampire are, "Why am I holding on to this vampire? What am I personally getting out of it?" The answer to both questions were that I was a major people pleaser and desperately wanted everyone and their mothers to like me.

How to Kill the People Pleaser in You

These scripts were constantly running in my head:

"If I don't please everyone in my life, they might not like me," and "If I don't do this for them, they won't love me anymore," and "Everyone else deserves to be taken care of before me."

Those thoughts are all a bunch of unicorn poop. If someone really loved and/or respected me, they would like me whether I did the things they asked of me or not. If they didn't, I was simply being used and taken advantage of.

There are so many reasons you may feel the need to people please, like:

Desiring praise to feel honored

Wanting a thank-you to feel appreciated

Craving validation to feel important

Doing something for someone so they won't leave you

The common thread is that they are all manipulations based on receiving a desired outcome.

I watched a reality television show recently (I know, a total time vampire and I'm working on it), and the star of the show had just read the gossip columns. The columnist had stated the star's clothes were terrible and that she needed to step it up when it came to her fashion. Buying into the idea that if she got the right clothes, she would be happy, the starlet went crazy, spending hundreds of thousands of dollars. On top of that, she was wasting so much of her precious time that she often complained about not having enough of.

The show never addressed the fact that she was throwing thousands of dollars out the window trying to please people. What should have been highlighted is that it doesn't matter what people think of you or your clothing choices. If you're doing you and you love your authentic style, it doesn't matter what anyone else thinks.

Life feels much more sweet when you stop caring about others' opinions.

In order to end your people-pleasing forever, you have to say no!

Just Say No. For Real This Time.

By not saying "yes" to every single thing anyone asks of you, you are practicing love and compassion for yourself and like we chatted about earlier, the entire Universe. Taking back your power over your time is essential. It's yours to do whatever you want with, so you might as well do some awesome shit with it.

Slay the Biggest Time and Energy Vampire of them All

Make sure you're getting enough good sleep. Exhaustion makes it extremely difficult to practice loving boundaries when it comes to letting those pesky vampires in. It may sound simple, but getting a good night's sleep is the most important thing you can do for yourself.

Four Ways to Sleep Your Way to the Top.

Make your bedroom a sanctuary. Bedrooms are for sleeping, cuddling, makin' sweet, sweet love, and nothing else. No exceptions. It's not a place for eating, exercising (unless it's sex-ercising), or watching television.

Remove everything that emits light from your bedroom. Your brain doesn't register it's night time if it's not completely dark, and you won't get true, restful sleep. I understand that alarm clocks are important, so if you have one, place a dark towel over it to dim the light. If for whatever reason you still can't get your room completely dark, get yourself a sleep mask to block out all the light. My sleep mask is my BFF and has changed my life, especially when traveling.

Shut down all electronics two hours before bedtime. Electronics fire up a whole bunch of parts of your brain and get your transmitters all riled up, making it scientifically harder to sleep.

Create a relaxing night-time ritual. Restorative yoga, reading, washing your face, lotion-ing yourself up, taking a bubble bath, or drinking some warm herbal tea are all great winding down activities.

Suggested Listening:

That's What's Up by Edward Sharpe and the Magnetic Zeros
Time is On My Side by the Rolling Stones
(Sittin' On) The Dock of a Bay by Otis Redding
I'm Right Here by Spencer Albee featuring Kat Wright
Time by Pink Floyd
Waste by Phish
More Interesting by Hayley Jane and the Primates

ROCK THE MAGIC!

Time and Energy Vampires:

What they are? How much time a week do you spend on them?

Vampire: _____ Time Spent: _____

Vampire: _____ Time Spent: _____

Vampire: _____ Time Spent: _____

Vampire: _____ Time Spent: _____

Vampire: _____ Time Spent: _____

Bonus points: Get off of social media for a day to a week and make some dates to hang with people in real life.

Super bonus points: Don't do any of the things you listed above and add up the time you saved. Give yourself a permission slip to do something you love with that time.

Writing Prompts

What and or who do you have a hard time saying no to and why?

How are you going to build up your 'no' muscle?

Reflections

6

TAKE THE HIGHWAY TO THE AWESOME ZONE

"Just remember that you're different
That should be sufficient
Making weird consistent
Know that you're significant"

Nature by Madaila

After nine months of using my inner wisdom to develop from a couple of cells into a baby in my mama's womb, I, being the genius that I was, knew how to make my way out into the world when the time was right even though my due date was 28 days prior to my grand entrance. My mom's a genius as well because she had never grown a human being in her body before and she, too, intuitively knew what to do. After that fateful day when I said, "hello world," and exited my mama, I evolved and grew up and the unique natural-born gifts I was born with started to show themselves.

In the self-help world, there's a huge emphasis placed on figuring out what your passion is and then taking it a step further to find a way to make money doing whatever that is. After reading all the books, I still couldn't figure it out. The books were taunting me by telling me I was basically a failure at life. Not wanting to be a loser, I forced myself to make something happen and when that backfired I ended up even more confused, exhausted and hopeless than before.

The failures kept on coming full speed ahead because I was constantly devising a plan on how to make money from my passions. Where did I go wrong? I made it all way too complicated and placed way too much emphasis on the result. I totally forgot that my only purpose was super duper simple.

It's to be me. The end.

Sounds great and all, but how can just being me be it? How am I going to support myself?

Finding the best (and most fun) avenue to deliver my brand of awesome to the world was the key. And without having attachment to what that looks like or putting all of my energy into, how it could possibly be a business sounds majorly counterintuitive. I know, but hear me out.

A woman who attended one of my retreats was an artist, but stopped creating art because she didn't know how to make money doing it.

She had tried a bunch of things and they didn't work, so she found herself with a job she sort of liked that paid the bills. Expressing that squashing her art making affected everything in her life negatively, she was at a loss as to what to do.

I simply said, "Go home and make art everyday. For five minutes. For 12 hours. I don't care. Just do it because you love it. That's the only reason you need. The rest will fall into place if you're open to it."

Love acting? Act. Love running? Run. Love live music? Go out and see live music. Love playing with your kids? Play with your kids.

The greatest ideas never happen when you try to force them to. Check out my story:

Feeling super frustrated, I held myself hostage in my office. I wasn't allowed freedom until I figured out what the next steps were in my business. Things were going slow and I was barely making a profit. I knew I had some awesome ideas that would change the world, but I didn't know how to get them out of me. Attempting to force them out with all my might, while feverishly working on my computer, didn't seem to be working. I slammed my laptop shut and went on a Phish Halloween run in Atlantic City instead.

Totally forgetting about my business, I surrendered fully into the experience that is a Phish concert. And that's when it hit me. I looked around at the crowd of tens of thousands of people when the light bulb went off. If even one percent of these people care at all about what I'm doing, I will be extremely successful.

I had been wanting to create online coaching programs, retreats, workshops, talks and write a book that had the live music fanatic in mind, but I talked myself out of it thinking that it was too small of a niche.

I had spent a couple of years working my ass off, offering programs to everyone and no one was buying. The reason? I wasn't speaking to anyone in particular so no one was listening.

Once I started focusing on live music fans who wanted to rock their lives, everything fell into place. I got to speak my native language (jamband) and my business not only became profitable, but it was so freakin fun too! And the people I was attracting were the best in the land. I get teary eyed just thinking about how lucky I am that I got to work with them.

If you know you have amazing gifts to give, but don't know exactly the avenue in which to deliver them, or you're stuck, or you just don't know what your next step is, my advice is always the same:

Go out and see live music. Immerse yourself in the scene. Phish is my way of channeling the Universe. What's yours?

Even after you've figured out how you're going to deliver your own personal brand of awesome to the world, it's an extremely common occurrence to get distracted and fall off course. It happened to me when writing this book. There were four titles of this book that didn't match the contents of the book before I landed on the perfect one. I got so distracted that I didn't see the title that was shouting at me all along.

It's easy to get stuck with a hypothetical flat tire on the side of the highway when you're doing all sorts of things that aren't in your awesome zone. You know the things I'm talking about. The ones that distract you from doing whatever it is that you're awesome at. The things you either suck at, are OK at, are really good at and even the ones you are the best at. What makes them not awesome zone activities are that they don't light you up. Instead of feeling motivated to rock them all day and all night, they exhaust you.

Stop doing those things. If they need to happen in order for your business to run or your life to thrive, delegate them if possible. Ask for help. Hire someone.

For example, let's look at an artist who needs a website to sell her work. Instead of hiring a professional, she attempts to do it herself even though she doesn't know the first thing about how to design a website. Totally frustrated, it takes her countless hours of time where she could have been creating more art. Hiring someone qualified to do the job, the site would be done in a fraction of the time, meaning more people would be able to purchase her art sooner. Even though there is a bigger initial investment to hire a professional, in the end would have saved her money.

Do whatever you can to live fully in your awesome zone today. You'll have so much more energy to deliver your brand of awesome in whatever avenue you choose to do it in.

I love to write, so I wrote. This book is one of the avenues I took to deliver me to you. Yay!

Stop driving yourself crazy. Your only purpose is to be you and you can be you doing anything. Even in that job you hate. By embracing your awesomeness, you may find that all the things that aren't in alignment (maybe even that job you hate) will get crowded out and replaced with all things magic. You'll never know if you don't put the wildest expression of your authentic self (which is your awesome zone) into your current situation.

What to Do if You've Lost Yourself:

Along the wild journey of life, I received many confusing messages that made me totally forget what I wanted to do with myself. Because of this messaging, I found myself lost, steering away from my passions and toward safe jobs that had great paychecks, but weren't fulfilling. Not only that, but I slowly stopped doing the things I loved because I simply didn't have the time or energy. Those jobs were distractions that distracted me so hard that, before I realized what was happening, my gifts were so shut down I couldn't remember what they were.

I found myself in jobs that I was the worst at, occupations I was kinda good at, and ones where I was the best in my field. They all had something in common though; each and everyone was their own unique soul-sucking demon because I was not utilizing my natural born gifts.

My parents (out of wanting the best for me because they love me) once said to me something like this: "It doesn't matter if you like your job or not, as long as it has health benefits. Most people don't like their jobs and that's life." I always questioned if that's how life was supposed to be.

I was constantly pondering these questions:

Was I put on this earth to work an insane amount of hours per week doing something I don't like just so I can get a decent paycheck and receive health benefits?

Am I here to work really hard at something during the prime of my life, so that

when I'm old, I can retire and THEN start living?

Is it better for me to play it safe and have a job that's secure, even if I don't feel fulfilled, than it is to take risks?

Does anyone really make money living a life of passion, purpose, and service?

Completely lost in the illusion of the American dream, I applied for and got the job as a dance teacher in a public school. Amazing health benefits and a steady paycheck were the whip cream on the 'everyone is going to think I made it' sundae. Money was getting put into a 401K and my parents were on cloud nine.

After the excitement from all the outside approval wore off, each day when I woke up and went to work, I dreaded it. I would get down on my knees and pray to get into a car accident on the way to work. When kids were sick, I would sit really close to them, hoping to get lucky and catch what they had before sending them to the nurse to go home. I injured my back badly, and the doctor told me that I couldn't go to work for a week, and I actually cheered in his office.

I cheered because I was excited I was so injured that I couldn't work. Is that what life's about? Are we just supposed to suffer day in and day out? Was I being a spoiled brat? I mean, I did have a "good job."

There will be people that will tell you that yes, you are being a spoiled brat and that suffering is all a part of adulting. Just because it is for them, doesn't mean it has to be for you.

If you can't or don't want to quit your job, try infusing a little bit of you and what makes you happy into your job. If that's not possible, try doing something you love during any down time you have. If you don't have any down time, do it while you're using the bathroom. I've been known to throw a raging dance party for one in the bathroom stall at my job.

Getting caught up in the American dream of success while becoming attached to how much stuff you have acquired, can cause you to get into careers and situations that you're not really too interested in, but have to keep because otherwise you'll lose all the stuff. How can you simplify your life, downsize what you currently have, while cutting down on the amount of money you spend on the stuff that isn't sparking happiness? When you have less stuff to worry about paying for, it's easier to take risks.

There's been something inside of you that's trying to tell you something extremely important. It's been talking to you since you were a kid and at one point you heard it and did what it said without much thought. And it was glorious! Until someone told you it was stupid and you shut it down. That person/people didn't know what they were talking about because your inner voice/guidance is and has always been a genius and knows what's up. Now that you're an adult the voice may be just a muffled whisper, but it's still there trying to get your attention. Start to listen to it as that voice is your most valuable consultant. Like millions of dollars an hour valuable. At least. Probably more.

In the song *The Rainbow Connection,* The Muppets tell it like it is.

I've heard it too many times to ignore it.
It's something that I'm supposed to be.
Someday we'll find it,
The rainbow connection,
The lovers, the dreamers, and me.

Put your hand on your heart and ask yourself these questions. Be open to the answers coming forward (no matter how crazy you think they are) because I like crazy.

"What lights me up?"
"What do I desire to share with others?"
"What could I do all day every day?"
"How can I be of service to others?"
"What does my heart want me to know right now?"
"What's the first step?"

It's time to channel your childlike wonder and do what your inner wisdom tells you without putting much thought into it. If you don't, you'll receive something so powerful it will knock your socks off and not in a good way. It's the dreaded Universal bitch slap. Yikes!

What the Heck Is a Universal Bitch Slap?

A Universal bitch slap happens when you don't pay attention to your inner intelligence and ignore all the signs you're given. Here's an example; in the same week, you lose your job, your significant other breaks up with you, you break your finger, your car breaks down in the rain in an area with no cell reception, the person who had tickets for you for that very in demand show screws you over by accidentally giving your ticket away to someone else, you get kicked out of your apartment, and your cat throws up inside your sneaker, which you don't notice until you put on the sneaker. The slapping (aka your inner wisdom doing its best to get you to open your eyes to the signs) gets harder and harder until you fall so hard it knocks the wind out of you and you have no other choice but to run away and lock yourself in a tall tower in the woods or make a change. Getting to the point of permanent hermit-dom is avoidable.

How to Avoid a Universal Bitch Slap:

Teach yourself to listen to your inner wisdom again. When you were a baby, you were awesome at it. Feeling hungry? Scream waaaaaaahhhhhhh and someone will come and feed you. Wet your pants? Scream waaaaaaahhhhhhh and someone will come and change your diaper. More than likely, as you grew up, your all knowing inner intelligence got shut down so many times that it got quieter and quieter until you it became barely a whisper.

Since the voice might be so quiet or even silent right now, start small. When you're at the grocery store, and you can't decide between the almond milk or the coconut milk, take three deep breaths and ask yourself, "Do I want almond milk or coconut milk?" Without putting any thought into it, just pick one.

Another way to wake up your inner genius is to think back to a time when you can remember hearing it loud and clear. It still counts whether you listened to it or not.

When you were a teenager and your friend pressured you to do something you didn't want to do, and you heard the voice or felt that gut feeling that told you not to do it, but you did it anyway and then got into a lot of trouble. That time you were driving and you knew you were supposed to get off at the next exit, but you questioned yourself and kept driving, missing the correct exit. When you went on a date with someone and you felt like you shouldn't go out with them again, but you did anyway and it didn't end well.

Or on the flip side: When you were at a restaurant and you looked at the menu and knew exactly what you wanted, ordered it, ate it, and it was sooooooo good. When your buddies tried to convince you to skinny dip in the ocean and you knew you shouldn't, so you didn't and their clothes, wallets, and phones all got washed away into the sea, never to be found again. And when you saw this book, purchased it and read it up until this point, loved it, and it changed your life. In all of those scenarios, that was your inner wisdom talkin'.

If your inner intelligence was shut down for most of your life, it will take some time get its voice back. The good news is that the more you listen and take the appropriate action, the louder it will get, the more you'll listen, and the result will be that the Universe will never bitch slap you again. Woohoo!

When you start to reconnect with your purpose in life to just be yourself, no matter how old you are, it will be easier to narrow down what you're truly amazing at. The fun part comes when you can start to play with how those skills can be a part of your life and your journey. Don't worry if you feel like what you want to do has been done before. There are no new ideas. It's all been done before, but the difference is, it's never been done by you.

> "There is no such thing as a new idea. It is impossible. We simply take a lot of old ideas and put them into a sort of mental kaleidoscope. We give them a turn and they make new and curious combinations. We keep on

turning and making new combinations indefinitely;
but they are the same old pieces of colored glass that
have been in use through all the ages."

~Mark Twain

Are you hiding behind being OK at everything?

It's time to hop on my magic rainbow time machine and take a little journey back to my high school days. I was standing on the stage in the auditorium, freaking out on the inside because I had to tell my easily angered, larger-than-life school play director that I had to leave rehearsal early to go to dance. I raised my hand and told him I had to leave. I'm pretty sure I saw steam burst out of his ears as he yelled, "Go!" Even though he was really mad at my leaving, he let me go because I didn't have a very big part in the show since I never showed that I was fully committed. You see, I was constantly leaving practice early. Running off the stage, down the stairs and out of the building at full speed, I dove head first into my mom's car to get sped off to my dance class that I was now late for.

I was always in trouble at dance, too, because I was late from being at cheerleading and play practices. I was a member of the Art, Photography, and Drama Clubs, on the student council, and participated in Math League. I was always missing something for something else or leaving early because I had to go to dance class, play practice, or cheerleading. I prided myself on the fact that I did so many things and was so well-rounded. The thing was, I was good at everything I did, but never gave myself the chance to be great at anything.

I was totally drained from doing so many things half-assed.

This genius scheme I concocted was the ultimate cover up. It was the perfect scapegoat for people not to notice that I was afraid to go big. Instead of going for anything for real, I played half-assed instead because it was safer. Being brutally honest, I never tried to be great at anything because the risk was too scary for me to handle. When I received mediocre results, I was happy because at least I didn't fail. But if I did happen to fail, that was ok in my mind because it was obviously a result of doing sooooo many things. It wasn't because I wasn't great. Oh, no! It was because I missed a rehearsal or a practice, or I was sick because I was over-tired, or whatever other excuse I came up with.

I continued this pattern during and after college by having a lot of jobs, all of which I showed up to half-assed. I was in a couple of dance companies and was always missing rehearsals to be at other rehearsals or to be at one of my other jobs. I taught dance. I was a singing telegram. I delivered pre-cooked steak dinners. I was a waitress. I did promotional work for beer, liquor, and chocolate companies. I was a data entry person at my dad's office. I choreographed and did costume design for school plays. And I had other jobs I'm probably forgetting. I was all over the place. Again, I was protecting myself, because if I were to fail at anything, it wasn't because I wasn't great. It was because I was too busy. It was a lie of epic proportions.

Finding myself with a tiny shovel in my hands and panting from digging a million small holes all over the place, I realized I was going nowhere. I was lost, exhausted, disappointed, defeated, and stuck and I didn't know what to do.

If you can relate to my story, I feel you. There's good news here though. The Universe has a funny way of letting you know it has your back. Remember in a previous chapter where I shared the story of my devastating career-ending injury when I was a professional cheerleader? At the time, I didn't know it, and I probably wouldn't have believed it even if you had told me, but that injury turned out to be one of the biggest blessings of my life.

Why was it such a blessing? My boyfriend at the time was at the game, saw me get hurt and went home without checking in on me. When I arrived home, I found him across the street at a bar. Instead of consoling me or giving me a shoulder to cry on, he told me my injury was my fault because I was the one who decided to be a professional cheerleader in the first place. During my recovery period, he wasn't emotionally or physically there for me the way I needed him to be and wondered how he would treat me if I had his baby or got seriously ill.

One day a friend told me about this amazing school called the Institute for Integrative Nutrition. After checking it out, my intuition screamed, "Go to that school!" I was like, "Whaaaaaat? How am I going to pay for it and make the time to go?" With childlike impulsivity, I signed up and it was one of the greatest investments I've ever made. While at school, I was taught that in order to be great at what I was doing and to use my gifts, I had to stop digging a million holes. Focusing my energy into digging one big giant beautiful hole, I finally started to get somewhere.

I stopped trying to force a life purpose and just starting living. Doing more yoga, going to more live music concerts and festivals, hiking in the great outdoors, making in-person dates with my friends, watching sunsets, and concocting delicious healthy meals were some of things I made a priority. Slowly, the unique gifts I had within me all along started to slowly emerge. All the things that happened in my life may have derailed me a little, but all of it brought me to this point in my life and I feel an immense amount of gratitude for it.

Everyone wants to be able to do work that uses their most awesome talents, and it's their birthright to do so. Don't get discouraged because you can't see the signs right now and you want the Universe to say to you, "Yo! You are doing the right thing, and here are the signs to let you know that's true."

You will get the signs. Be patient and trust. It all unfolds with Divine timing. It's coming. I can feel it.

Suggested Listening:

Danger Zone by Kenny Loggins
Vienna by Billy Joel
The Zone by The Weeknd
Space Oddity by David Bowie
Banana Pancakes by Jack Johnson
This Little Light of Mine by the Staple Singers

ROCK THE MAGIC!

It's great to have a lot of interests, but it's important to be mindful that your interests aren't diluting your awesome. Which ones help you bring your brand of awesome into the world and which ones distract you?

Write down the ones that build up your awesome.

What can you do this week to incorporate all of that into your life in a practical way?

Writing Prompts

Write about a time you heard your inner guidance loud and clear, but didn't listen.

Write about a time you did.

Reflections

7

BECOME A MANIFESTING UNICORN

"*I'm just sitting here watching the wheels go round and round*
I really love to watch them roll
No longer riding on the merry-go-round
I just had to let it go"

Watching the Wheels by John Lennon & Yoko Ono

One fine day, someone found a piece of gold and decided it was more valuable than the other rocks and stones. Throughout the history of the world, currency has come in many different forms, such as shells, cattle, camels, salt, parmigiano cheese, squirrel pelts, and sacks of cereal grains. Nowadays, money is mostly electronic. What money symbolizes is an exchange of energy. You work; you receive energy in the form of money, and you then spend, invest and save that money.

At the root of all things is evil. Just kidding! It's energy. Everything around you, from the paper in this book to the ink used to print these words to the eyes used to read them—all are forms of energy. When you figure out how to use it to your advantage, you can change your reality, thus becoming a manifesting unicorn.

If you're waiting for all your manifestations to come flying in full speed on a rainbow smack dab into your life, the first action you must take is to believe you deserve everything you desire and more. I failed to see my potential because I perceived myself as a scatterbrained, always-with-the-wrong-man failure of a woman who was unworthy of great things.

I was blind to the truth in the same way one might be blind to ever experiencing love again after they've just had their heart broken into a million pieces. The pain is so debilitating that they're unable to imagine feeling like him or herself again. Just like that person couldn't imagine a world where they could possibly experience a loving relationship again, I couldn't picture one where I had it together, was with a man who adored me as much as I adored him, loved myself and felt successful.

Then I caught a tiny glimpse of it and saw that what I desired could actually be real. After years of figuratively wandering the streets, to make a long story short, I found what I was looking for, and it was there within me all along.

As a youngster, I felt a deep compassion for those who were struggling, and I enjoyed finding ways to make their lives easier. My friends, and even strangers, naturally trusted me and felt safe to share their deepest, darkest secrets that had never before seen the light of day. If I wasn't able to help, I reveled in connecting them with someone who could. My smile was contagious and my favorite healing tool. Being a total weirdo myself and owning it, my friends often found themselves doing fun and strange things with me they never thought they'd do.

All of the above, the retreats I host and even this book are not my gift, but they are the avenues in which I get to deliver it. Finding an avenue where I could be me in all of my gloriousness was the key factor in my success. Even though I experienced a lot of failures along the way, I was able to imagine what was possible for me.

After I accomplished a little success, I started to feel like a total badass and took crazy risks that led to me hosting retreats all over the world, getting booked to speak at events, moving to Vermont without knowing anyone besides the man I had been dating for less than thirty days, and marrying a super hot stud-muffin with the biggest heart. I honestly and truly love my life today! I'm not sharing this to brag about how awesome I am, but to show that if this Negative Nelly can do it, anything's possible.

Having spent so many years with negative thoughts reigning over my brain, making space for new, positive thoughts felt like a huge undertaking. But I wanted to be a manifesting unicorn, so I did it. Manifesting is not sitting at home, wishing for something and then having it appear like magic. (Even though sometimes it works that way and it would be awesome if it always worked that way.) It takes a creative imagination, elbow grease and a whole lotta gratitude for what you have right now.

"You want to know the difference between a master and a beginner? The master has failed more times than the beginner has ever tried." ~Yoda

Stuff that Tries to Knock You Off Your Manifesting Unicorn Saddle

Getting stuck in your noggin

When you focus completely on what you're thinking about and your head is full of negative thoughts, forcing happy ones in will do nothing for you besides leave you frustrated. It's a trap!

Feeling icky when you think about what you want doesn't work either. On the contrary, when you feel good, it does work. Instead of trying with all your might to force good thoughts into your head, stop, and actually, physically do something that makes you feel good instead. The better you feel, the higher your vibration, and like magic you'll start attracting happier thoughts and things.

Losing motivation when nothing's happening

When you're manifesting stuff into your life with ease and you're in the flow, it feels amazeballs. Shouting from the rooftops so everyone can hear you that this manifesting thing works is something you can't help doing. Until it feels like the flow stops for a few hours, days or months. Your perception is that nothing is happening, and even though a bunch of good stuff already happened for you, amnesia sets in, and you forget all about it. Thinking that it's all a bunch of unicorn poop puts you onto the path of a vicious cycle.

The best anti-venom you can take for this predicament is working on feeling good for no other reason than just because. Refer back to the Self-Care Superhero and Get High chapters.

Believing the non-believers

If you're a manifesting virgin, your old way of thinking and being are holding on with all their might. The old and new are having a tug of war with your head and even one more person on the other team (aka a non-believer trying to convince you it's all a bunch of BS) will send you into the late night ditch party where things are starting to get shady and not in a good way. Living as a Manifesting Unicorn is a radical way of being and may cause some people to feel very triggered.

You're still reading, so this concept has resonated with you at least a little bit. Some magical things may have already happened in your life that prove to you that this manifesting thing is real. But at the same time, you might still have a little (or a lot) of doubt sneaking its way into your subconscious, and the last thing you need is someone getting into your head adding more doubt.

How to Know You're Doing it Right (AKA Noticing the Signs)

You're feelin good

When you take your 'how good am I feeling' temperature, and you've got the fever, it's a huge sign that this manifesting thing is working for you. Since you attract stuff based on how you feel in any given moment, the better you're feeling, the more you're aligned with the things you want. I like to think that even if it doesn't work (which it does), the worst thing that could possibly happen is that you feel better.

When life is flinging fake concert tickets at you, it's even more important to do whatever you can to feel a little joy. The more you practice this, the less resistance you'll have to allow yourself to do the things that tickle your fancy.

Have fun along the journey and be mega patient and open to things happening in unexpected ways. Since what you're doing is actually attracting a feeling that you'll have from acquiring whatever it is you desire, in the big scheme of things, the specific outcome doesn't really matter.

You hit bumps in the road

Obstacles can knock even the most badass of unicorns off their motorcycle. For me, when things aren't working out in the most magical way that I built up in my head, I start to wonder if it's even working out at all. Remembering it's all a part of the process and even a sign that I'm on the right path, I stand back up, dust myself off, and keep going. Lessons I still need to learn are often hidden in the obstacle that I need to get before I ease on down the road.

Other times the roadblock is there because there are still things in my life I need to let go of to make room for what I desire; these roadblocks force me to get rid of something that I'm too afraid to get let go of myself. Like when I couldn't admit that someone wasn't the right fit for me, and then they broke my heart. Sometimes I forget what a powerful manifesting machine I am even while it's happening.

It's slow flowin'

Sometimes your manifestations won't show up all at one time like all the mail order tickets for the summer tour that you scored in the ticketing lottery. Instead, they might happen over time, like finding single tickets sporadically. This occurs because you can't handle it all happening at once. It's like wanting to have five children and then finding out you are pregnant with quintuplets.

The signs are flirting with you

Sometimes you'll receive little teasers of manifestations to help you know that what you want isn't just a pipe dream, but a real possibility. You'll notice stuff you didn't notice before. If you want to go see your favorite band's concert in Mexico, for instance, you'll start to see symbols of the country, you'll hear it mentioned in the news, and you'll meet people who have been there before or are going this year. Those signs are showing up to show you that you're on the path to finally allow it to happen.

It's *mostly* right, but...

These sneaky little bastards can throw you for a loop. You're presented with an opportunity that's pretty close to what you're looking for, but something about it isn't exactly quite right.

For example, you receive an offer for gig you've been dreaming about for years, but they don't have a budget to pay you. You put in an offer on your dream home, but you find out after your inspection is complete that the roof is leaking and it has termites.

You're presented with a big decision to make. You may wonder, is this the opportunity I've been waiting for? Does it look different than I thought, or is it a test to see if I am brave enough to let that opportunity go to make room for the best case scenario? Eeeeeeek! So confusing.

Since you're the king/queen bee, you hold the magical decision wand. Something you need to know that will make this a little less stressful is to become keen to the fact that Eminem was wrong. You're never only given one shot. Just like how the cheap tequila gets thrown back at all inclusive resorts, the shots are limitless. Make a choice, go for it, and if it ends up being the wrong decision, make a different one.

In the case of the gig with no budget, will it get you in front of a large audience? Is the exposure worth the no pay? When you think about taking advantage of the opportunity, how does it feel? If you feel icky, pass because it's an *almost manifestation*. If you feel good, do it! Remember this whole manifesting thing is based on how good you feel and if you feel good, it's never wrong.

How to Circulate Money with Integrity

It's much harder to shine your light when you can't pay your light bill.

What does it mean to circulate money/energy consciously and with integrity? It means spending money on people, places and things that have integrity while at the same time earning your money with integrity. If you purchase items from companies who treat employees poorly, or test on animals, or utilize child labor, or use dangerous chemicals, realize that your dollars are supporting that. Dollars are extremely powerful, and no matter how many of them you have, you can make a difference in the way you use them, so use them wisely.

Paying bills is an activity that most adults must do, and do often, yet it is one of the most dreaded. Would it be possible to make bill paying a feel good activity? What if, after you complete payment for each bill, you expressed gratitude for the service or product you received? For example, instead of thinking, "Are you kidding me? This heating bill is going to be the end of me," you think, "I'm so grateful for the abundance I have to use toward heating my home, making it a comfortable place to be for me and my family."

When I feel closed off to the limitless abundance that surrounds me, it's often because I fear there is a lack of whatever it is that I want. I sometimes think, "There isn't enough for me." Lack of money, love, trust, resources, worthiness, or having enough are the most common fears people have. Unless you start practicing gratitude, you'll find yourself stuck in Lack Canyon with no ladder, ropes, or cell service, no matter how hard you try to manifest.

You deserve to be just as wealthy as the next guy. Keep believing, continue to take action, say yes to receiving, and never stop being grateful for whatever it is you have right now.

Still feeling stuck?

The ground rules of abundance

Rocking your abundance is easy if you follow these rules.

Say yes to the things that feel good; say no to the things that don't.

Have an attitude of gratitude.

Chill. Breathe.

Have fun on a daily basis.

Practice self-care.

Circulate your money with integrity.

Give big.

Receive big.

Love big.

Now that you know everything you need to know to become a Manifesting Unicorn, let's talk about money and why it's important that you have it.

You're a good person, right? If you had a huge pile of money, you would do amazing things with it, true? And with that money, so many people would be helped, fact? So your prosperity would prosper others, correct? Well, that's why it's really damn important that you have money.

"I can't afford that" was one of my most used sayings. Something occurred to me. What if instead of saying, "I can't afford that," I said, "I choose not to spend my money on that." Manifesting relies heavily on how you're feeling at any given moment, and declaring that I couldn't afford something felt disempowering and sad. Choosing not to invest my money in something gave me my power back because I was the one in charge of the choice. Instead of "I can't," I knew that I could, but "I chose not to."

Let that Shit Go! Here's How:

Fears

Receiving the limitless abundance that is available to you isn't possible if you're holding onto the stories and beliefs from your past that don't support your new way of being. Fear is usually the star of the show. What are you REALLY afraid of? Could it possibly be that you're afraid of what happens when you succeed? Or that you fear that money is evil? Or you believe you don't deserve it? Or you're afraid that you'll get it and lose it? Or maybe you just don't think you can be trusted with it?

Imagine what would happen if all of your fears came to fruition. What would your life really be like? My biggest fear was if I took risks and invested in myself and my dreams I would find myself homeless and starving if it didn't work. The real truth of my worst case scenario (and I'm aware of how lucky I am) was not me wandering the streets without a home or food to eat. Even if I risked it all and "lost everything," my loved ones would take me in. Most of the time, the real worst case scenario plays out way worse in your head. And then there's the possibility of the best case scenario happening. How epically amazing that would be? To me, it's almost always worth it to risk the worst case scenario coming true for a chance at living the best one.

Regrets

Regrets are the next weasels that can be responsible for sneaking their way into your being and messing with your abundance mojo. What "could have been" is a projection of what you think life could be like, but it's not reality.

All the things you've ever been through in your life have brought you to where you are today. All your choices (the smart and the not so smart ones) are a part of you. You may be dealing with the repercussions of your past choices, but the good news is today is a new day, and you can do whatever you want with it.

Doubts

I remember desperately wanting to be a cool kid when I was in the fifth grade. One day I felt courageous, so I strutted my tiny little legs across the playground until I found myself playing with the popular girls. So excited about what was happening, I thought to myself, "Tara! They like you. They really like you. You're the coolest cat in all the land!" After about a minute of bliss, one girl noticed something that didn't belong, and that something was me. She looked me dead in the eyes and said, "Tara, go play somewhere else." Devastated and embarrassed, trying to hide the tears streaming down my crimson red face, I ran away with my tail between my legs to find a hidden spot behind a tree to cry my eyes out.

For years, this playground story repeated itself in many different ways. If I was always being annoying and not wanted around, why would anyone choose to work with me when there were so many other coaches out there who were way more awesome than I was? Situations continued to manifest themselves, proving that all to be true, and they didn't stop until I forgave myself for buying into all the misunderstandings that started that day on the playground.

I took up residency at the poor house because I was protecting myself from reliving that awful feeling ever again. I let my fears, regrets, and doubts keep me from being awesome. I thought I was being kind to the world by not allowing myself to get out there, but I was really being selfish. My fear of rejection was so strong that I let it be the supreme ruler of my actions. Feeling that fear but finally having the courage to act, no matter the outcome, is still one of the scariest things ever. But I do it anyway. I do it for those who can't right now in the hopes that my actions may inspire them some day.

If you refuse to let go of your fears, your regrets, and your doubts, you're being selfish as well, because you're not going to going to give your best, most genuine self to yourself, your friends, family, co-workers, or the world. We all need you! Please don't suppress all of your amazing gifts and deny us the benefit of your awesomeness.

You've had these manifesting tools all along, you just needed to be reminded of them! Now go use them to your advantage. Just like Dorothy in the Wizard of Oz, you've always had the power to go home and make your dreams a reality.

Suggested Listening:

Songbird by Ryan Montbleau
Jump Into the Fire by Marco Benevento
Money by Pink Floyd
The Unicorn by the Irish Rovers
The Magical Mystery Tour by the Beatles
24K Magic by Bruno Mars

ROCK THE MAGIC!

How does money enrich your life?

List your reasons. Examples: I love money because it allows me to go to concerts. I love money because it allows me to travel. I love money because it allows me to donate to charities I believe in. I love money because it allows me to feed myself healthy food.

Get a clear idea of what you really want. Pick one thing you want to manifest in your life (like an apartment).

It must have (What are your non-negotiables?)

It would be really cool if it had (Dream big!)

What it must not have.

Create a Rock Your Life Board

Gather a bunch of magazines. Choose images that provoke a feeling that you desire and cut them out. Arrange them on a piece of poster board and glue them in place. With markers, write down words or phrases that spark positive feelings in you. Display your board where you can see it. Look at it everyday, close your eyes, and allow yourself to feel all the feels in that moment.

Under your Rock Your Life Board, write down what you can do to feel that way today. Repeat every day until it all comes true. If your feelings change about something on your board, take it off and replace it with something that feels good.

Writing Prompts

If someone sent you a check for $1,000,000, how would you spend it?

Reflections

8

FEEL ALL THE FEELS

"Now listen to the words I'm saying
In this line that your life will be just fine
And troubles do not stay
They get replaced with good times
Now you got a great life
Smile as you walk by
Thinking about the day"

When It Rains It Pours by Twiddle

Confession time. This chapter wasn't in the first draft of the book because it's a difficult subject I tried to avoid at all costs. Putting on my big girl sparkly panties, I got down to business and wrote what I feel is one of the most important and helpful sections of this book. And it wasn't easy or pretty because I spent a lot of time feeling ALL the feels (not just the warm fuzzy feeling kind). When I came out at the other end, I felt in my whole being that it was worth the effort and that the benefits far outweighed the massive uncomfortableness I experienced along the way.

Finding myself stuck in a deep dark funk, I figuratively and literally closed the curtains to the outside world. Some days I didn't brush my teeth or eat until it was dark out. Other days I wouldn't leave the couch. Opting out of the activities that brought me peace of mind — yoga, going out to see live music, and my daily walk into town to bring my hubster Dan his lunch — was starting to become my new normal.

Even though I forced myself to participate in enjoyable activities with friends, it felt like the dark cloud that was stalking me would sometimes hide for a moment, but the second I was alone, it was back again. While the cloud was fully enveloping me, I met a good friend of mine for lunch. He took one look at me, knew I wasn't ok, and asked me how I was. Avoiding eye contact, with a big fake smile on my face, I said I was fine and nervously giggled because I was worried he would find out my big secret that I wasn't happy.

Seeing right through my lies he asked me again if I was ok. I couldn't hide it anyway so I admitted the truth. He said, "I know. I see you and I love you and your sadness."

Reaching out to another friend for help out from the dark side, she sternly said, "Dudette! When I was feeling this way, you told me to allow yourself to feel all the feels. Sit in the dark, feel it all, really go there and don't make it right or wrong. Just allow it to be and see what happens. That's how I got out of my funk and that's how you'll get out of yours too."

I hate it (translation: I love it and am secretly super grateful for it) when my own advice is thrown back into my face. But dammit! I was right.

Another friend said to me, "When life gives you shit that's not a bad thing. Sit in it for a bit because it's the fertilizer that makes you grow!"

While I was embracing the darkness by sitting in all my shit, I wanted to stay hiding under the fuzzy blankets in my bed. Instead I made myself do the tiniest things to feel even a smidge better. To my surprise, it made a world of difference and slowly I started to get my mojo back. Because I felt a smidge better, I was able to tackle what I was unable to before. The poop I was sitting in stopped stinking so strongly until it wasn't even a skid mark and I started to sprout. I opened my curtains and let the light back in (figuratively and literally), put on sparkly booty shorts, listened to the songs *Sparkle* by Phish, *75 and Sunny* by Ryan Montbleau and *Shakedown Street* by the Grateful Dead on repeat, made myself my favorite healthy breakfast, brushed my teeth, and started to feel like myself again. Feeling like myself was a feeling that seemed impossible only days earlier.

How to Feel All the Feels

As humans we experience all kinds of feelings, yet some of them are considered wrong by society. Anger, sadness, fear, anxiety, grief and hopelessness are just some of them, and many of us have been told things like, "don't cry," "you're over emotional," or "just get over it already." There are many ways to hide your true feelings from being shown. Drinking alcohol, taking drugs, binging on food, having one-night stands, or purchasing stuff you don't need are all ways to numb your feels, give you a fast high to feel good for a sec, or hide them from coming to the surface all together. You may find it works for a little while. Until it doesn't and the time bomb that was ticking away inside of you finally goes off. You may find yourself punching a wall, picking a fight with a stranger, having a mental breakdown, in rehab, morbidly obese or ridden with disease.

Throughout my life, I stifled my emotions to protect those around me. I truly believed it was unsafe to be emotional and I didn't want to burden people with my problems, so I hid them away. Crying in front of people was a shameful act, so I always choked back my tears. I meant well, but it didn't do me or anyone else much good because I had uncontrollable temper tantrums well into my teens. During my college years, I suffered major digestive issues while battling one illness or another, and in my twenties I allowed an abusive man to be my boyfriend for over four years. Those were just some of the symptoms that showed up because of my emotion dodging.

Instead of allowing myself to drown in the emotion ocean, I needed to learn how to surf the wave.

I named all my feelings and treated them as if they were my friends instead of my enemies. Angry Adele, Worried Wilson, Sad Sade, Fearful Fergy, Anxious Amos, Happy Henrietta, Annoyed Annie, Joyful Jerry, Pissed Off Paul and Peaceful Patsy are some of my besties. My BFFs had a lot of messages to share with me that I had ignored in the past. Angry Adele told me to take action instead getting taken advantage of again. Sad Sade told me to cry it out, slow down, and give myself time to heal.

My emotions would hide in my neck, belly and lower back, so I knew when they were acting up, I was hiding something. Once I felt something physically, I would feel the sensation without judging it, making it good or bad, or making it mean something. Eventually the pain would fizzle out instead of manifesting into a full-blown ailment.

Instead of avoiding my feelings at all costs, I felt my way through them because all of those feels had some major wisdom within them just waiting to drop. When I can't shake a feeling, I ask it what it wants me to know. If my mind is too busy to get an answer, I'll go for a walk, meditate, dance or do some yoga. Once I feel even a little peace, the answer often reveals itself. I've started to listen to it, even if I don't like what it has to say, and I've learned so much.

This practice of feeling all the feels instead of letting them fester inside of me was a key move I made that turned my life from a shit storm to a rainbow sparkle party. After all, rainbows only happen after it rains. Funks still show up once in awhile, but I know how to get out of them so they aren't so debilitating and they don't last as long.

Sometimes the feelings you're experiencing aren't even your own. If you define yourself as a sensitive empath, chances are you're lugging around other people's emotions too. Being one myself, I have a couple of tools in my box I use to empty the duffle bag full of other people's feels I carry around with me. I picture a disco ball in front of me. I visualize all the emotions that aren't mine and I put them in that disco ball. I pretend to grab it with my hands, toss it into the air, and watch it spin so fast that everything inside of it it transforms into glitter that rains down on me. A second tool I use is to take a shower and picture everyone's emotions washing off of me and I watch them go down the drain.

Why Feelings are Confusing Bastards

It's totally possible and an extremely common occurrence to experience a bunch of emotions all at the same time that all contradict each other. For example, you might feel excited and fearful or happy and scared all at the same time. Another way feelings are sneaky sallys is they hide themselves behind other feelings hoping you won't notice they're there. Like when you feel angry, but the truth is you're not really angry. You're actually really freakin hurt.

Oftentimes, the more powerful of the two emotions hides behind the others ones because it's terrifying to express the stronger one. It's common to use the secondary emotion to mask what's really going on because it feels safer.

What to Do when Your Feelings are Playing Hide and Go Seek

For most people, expressing anger is actually much easier than letting someone know they've hurt you or that you're afraid of losing them. Anger is a wall that folks build to protect themselves from being vulnerable. The wall needs to be penetrated because the magic is discovered when you find the courage to express the hurt. That's when real intimacy is created.

Let's say you're totally freakin out about your job and when you get home, all you want is a supportive hug from your lover. When you get there and your partner is preoccupied with something else, instead of asking for a hug that more than likely they would gladly give you, you snap and say something snarky like, "You're never there for me you asshat."

Picking a fight with your partner is more than likely not going to get you that hug you so desire. What will more than likely happen is you'll push them away or trigger them to react with anger right back at ya. Expressing that you're super stressed by your work and all you need is a hug, if your partner is supportive of you, you'll totally get that hug.

The Dangers of Bottling it All Up

Our brains are amazing. When experiencing an extremely traumatic event such as being the victim of a violent crime or a car accident, our subconscious minds go into mama bear protection mode and turn our emotion switches to off. On the other hand, suppressing your emotions on purpose when you're not experiencing a major trauma can lead you down a destructive health path.

Avoiding your emotions won't make them dissolve into nothing and disappear. In fact it often has the opposite effect and makes them build up and get stronger and stronger until eventually you can't take it anymore and explode. For example, you are sad because your boyfriend broke up with you and is now dating your best friend and you pretend that you're totally fine with it even though you're not totally fine with it, and then you flip out at the person who accidentally lightly brushes your arm while dancing at a show. The outburst is your body doing its thing and trying to protect itself by looking for any excuse it can get to let that emotion out. This often leads to unnecessary overreactions over something unrelated and often unimportant.

The research says that constantly suppressing your emotions over time can cause high blood pressure, heart disease, stiff joints, and more illness due to a lowered immune system. Top that off with more anxiety and depression, and you've got a major problem on your hands.

Expressing your emotions in all their glory might not always be appropriate though. Like screaming really loud when you're at a seated listening room concert because you got a mean text from someone. Instead of reacting in the moment, take a few deep breaths and find a time and a place as soon as possible to express your emotions in a healthy way.

How to Allow Your Emotions to Keep Their Cool

There are some practices you can adopt to help you manage your emotions when you feel like a tea kettle about to blow. The first steps are to pause, take three breaths, and think before you act. We often get ourselves in trouble when we act abruptly.

When you're feeling super powerful emotions it's really hard to think rationally. Calming down is essential to think clearly and to see the situation for what it is and what emotion you're really feeling. Get outside and go for a walk, excuse yourself and take a breather, or, if you're at home, take it out on your pillow.

The next step is to process and identify the feel that you're actually feeling.

Remember that some feelings like to hide behind other feelings. Check yourself before you wreck yourself and dive into what the underlying emotions are that you're avoiding. Why are you feeling the way you are? What's it really about? Once you've figured that out you can decide the best way to move forward.

Suggested Listening:

Feeling Alright by Joe Cocker
No Rain by Blind Melon
Dead Set by Ryan Montbleau
I Feel It All by Feist
True Colors by Cyndi Lauper
I Will Follow You Into the Dark by Death Cab for Cutie
Flashdance...What a Feeling performed by Irene Cara

ROCK THE MAGIC!

Give a name to each of your feelings.

Make your feelings into an art project. Draw them into cartoons. Be sure to include a thought bubble with each one's most commonly used catch phrases.

Shake everyone else's feelings off. Put the feelings you know aren't yours inside the disco ball by writing each one of them in.

Next, shake this book with vigor to get them all out!

Bonus points: Play your favorite disco song, shake your sweet ass, and dance everyone's feelings off.

Writing Prompts

Write a letter to one (or more) of your feeling friends.

Write a dialog play between your feeling friends. Ask them questions and have them tell stories.

Reflections:

9

STOP BEING AN ASS

"Sink just below all the churning and froth
and swim to the light-source, or fly like a moth
so toss away stuff you won't need in the end
but keep what's important - and know who's your
friend"

Theme From the Bottom by Phish

If you think everyone in your life is an ass, chances are you're probably an ass too.

Do your friends have different morals than you, participate in activities you don't believe in, complain all the time, and love being miserable? If so, something's gotta change, because your friends are your mirror—a direct reflection of you.

When I'm having difficulty with this subject, which, as a spiritual being having a human experience, I sometimes do, I think about something my pastor friend Rachel Fraumann's father shared that helped me gain a better understanding on the subject.

There are two types of people in this world: frogs and crabs. Crabs have a hard exterior that's almost impossible to crack. When crabs are put in a bucket together, they pull their fellow crabs down from the top of the bucket. Helping another crab is out of the question because they believe it threatens their chances of getting out of the bucket themselves. It's a crab-against-crab world.

Crab-like people believe there isn't room for them to succeed if others are succeeding. They aren't keen to the fact that life affords the room for every person to have the opportunity to thrive if they work together toward a common goal. Watch out if you find yourself in a crab-like person's path. They'll use everything they've got to take you down, literally and/or figuratively, depending on the situation. There's always a winner and a loser.

Frogs are a totally different brand. When you put a bunch of frogs in a bucket, their main goal is the same as the crabs'. Unlike crabs though, frogs work together to escape by piling one on top of the other until every frog easily hops out of the bucket. It takes a village, and frog-like people are more than willing to be your village people.

What types of people are in your life as friends, coworkers, and family members? If you answered crab-like, you're likely a little crabby yourself. Start to consciously surround yourself with more frog-like folks while acting more froggy yourself.

And who wants crabs anyway? I know I didn't want to catch them from boys when I was in college, and I don't want them in my life now.

In chapter 5, I'll discuss how you can take steps every day to reach your goals and how, in order to do that, it requires a dream team. Keep in mind that your dream team should consist entirely of frog-like friends, mentors, and advisors.

Don't Save the Drama for Anyone, Not Even Your Mama

Hi. My name is Taraleigh and I'm a recovering drama-aholic.

She was mad at him because of something he said to her that he heard from a friend who told a friend who heard it from me. There was always something dramatic going on and I somehow found myself smack dab in the center of it. Drama was something I was constantly trying to stay out of, but how hard was I really trying if I was always caught up in it?

Drama is extremely exciting and highly addictive. Whether you are the one dishing out the drama or you are on the receiving end, you are the problem. The time has come to get radically honest and give yourself a big ol' bitch slap of reality. Let's kill your pesky drama habit for realsies this time.

Someone once asked me, "What are you getting out of the drama?"

At first I was like, "Yo, lady. I'm not getting anything out of the drama. It just happens. It's not my fault." She was like, "You are getting something out of it. Otherwise, you wouldn't be creating it or allowing it into your life." Duh! She was right, and I was embarrassed to admit it.

What was I getting from the drama? Actually, lots of things.

I was always sooooooo busy "fixing" everyone else's stuff, I had nooooooo time to work on my own stuff.

My life wasn't all unicorns and sparkles like I wanted it to be perceived, and I was embarrassed. I chose to lie to others and myself, which created more and more dramatic situations. I wasn't happy, so causing the suffering of others made me feel better. I felt stuck in my relationships and career so I would create dramatic situations to get out of them without having to do the dirty work myself.

If you're stuck in the troves of drama like I was, it doesn't mean you're a jerk, but it's time to stop acting like one.

Even though I tried to avoid it like I avoid dairy, high fructose corn syrup, and music venues where you're not allowed to dance, I had to look at why I was acting like such a jerk. I forced myself to dive deep into the scary dark places to find out what I was avoiding by bringing drama into my life. I didn't like what I saw, but it was a part of me. Sabotaging everything worked for me for a short amount of time, but then it imploded.

Forced to take action, I faced my demons head on and made some massive changes. It wasn't easy. In fact it was was really freakin hard, but worth it.

Stop Acting Like a Jerk. Here's How:

The best way to stop attracting jerks into your life is to practice radical kindness. The more I did it, the easier it became, until eventually being kind was second nature. Some side effects are most people respond to kindness with kindness and you'll experience a helper's high.

When you do something good for someone else, your brain's pleasure centers ignite like a fourth of July fireworks display. Some say when you do something nice for another living being, a group of living beings or for the world because you're in it for the helper's high, it's actually selfish and egotistical. I say, "Who cares?!?" You have more energy to do the things that give you pleasure than the stuff you hate or feel obligated to do, so if everyone did good deeds simply because they wanted to and it felt good, way more acts of kindness would happen.

Here are some simple ways you can spread kindness in the world:

1. Compliment someone on their beautiful smile or nice outfit or cool hair or fun shoes.

2. If you see someone struggling with their grocery bags, help them.

3. Miracle someone with a concert ticket (if you forget what it means to miracle someone please refer to chapter three).

4. Let the person in line behind you with one item go before you.

5. Hold the door for the person behind you.

6. Donate your time or money to a cause you believe in.

7. Make a meal for someone who is struggling, can't afford food or is just really busy.

8. Purchase a yoga class, a massage, a haircut, or a concert ticket for someone who could use one.

9. When you're out shopping (at the mall or on Shakedown Street) and you see something that someone you know would love, get it for them.

10. Pick up trash when you see it on the ground and throw it away.

Is Your Ego Being a Bitch?

Here's how to know:

Do you whine more often than not? Do find yourself playing the victim card hoping to get sympathy? Are you dressing in a way just so other people think you look smokin? Have you ever made up a sickness or injury for attention? Did you ever put another person down to feel better about yourself? Have you ever ghosted out on someone instead of telling them how you truly feel?

If you answered no, you're probably lying, you're not human, or you're fully enlightened. If you're like the rest of us and you answered yes, your ego was being super bitchy.

Sometimes, my ego gets so loud it's hard to hear myself think or feel. Since she wouldn't shut the hell up no matter how hard I meditated, I decided I was going to name her Sheila and start listening to what she had to say.

When Sheila is speaking to me and I ignore her completely, she takes over, and I start acting like a total ass. I don't like it when I act like a total ass (and neither does anyone else) so instead of continuing down that road, I sit down and have a heart-to-heart with her. (I do this by writing in my journal or by talking to myself.)

Oftentimes Sheila just needs a moment to process whatever hurt her. I let her know I hear her. She's just acting out because of the hurt she's endured throughout the years. Sheila's afraid she's going to experience the same hurt all over again. I assure her that this time is different and she may chill out, relax, and be quiet, because I'm stronger now. Even if I do end up getting hurt, it's ok. I'm willing to risk it in order to love bigger. My heart and soul are going to step in and take over now. Because of the acknowledgement, Sheila feels heard and knows she's safe to quiet down so I can hear what my heart is trying to tell me.

Sheila loves to rock out (just like me), and sometimes the best way to quiet her (otherwise known as getting out of my head and into my heart) is to dance.

Ego-Dance Party Tunes:

Oh Sheila by Ready for the World
Ego Trippin' at the Gates of Hell by Flaming Lips
Gangsta Like Me by Snoop Doggy Dog
The Glamorous Life by Sheila E
Ego by Beyoncé featuring Kanye West
Love Me Two Times by The Doors
Sexy and I Know It by LMFAO
Anything by Touchpants

Are You a Spiritual Hooligan?

Instead of taking responsibility for your actions, have you ever used new age jargon to manipulate the situation to your benefit to get yourself out of almost anything, to play the victim, to get what you want, to hurt others, or to excuse your bad behaviors. If so, you're spiritual bypassing which makes you a spiritual hooligan. Here's some specific examples of spiritual shenanigans:

You stroll up without a care in the world to meet your friend two hours later than you said you would meet them. Justifying that you've done nothing wrong because you were simply surrendering to the flow and running on the divine timing of the Universe, you believe that your tardiness and not sending them a text or calling wasn't your fault. You expect your friend to accept this explanation as a valid reason, so you tell them chill out and trust that the Universe wouldn't let you get hurt when they express how they were freaking out thinking you were dead in a ditch.

Your boyfriend/girlfriend suspects that you've been cheating on him with your ex. Being the intuitive person your significant other is, he/she eventually wears you down and pries the truth out of you. You explain how banging your ex was the most loving act for all involved because now all three of you can truly move on. Now that everyone has closure, there's more room for you to love your man/woman. You assure him/her that you did it for him/her and that he/she should feel honored by your great sacrifice.

You're acting like a jerk to everyone in your life. Claiming it's just who you are because of the astrological sign you were born under, you don't try to make changes.

Feeling really pissed off that an opportunity you were pining over went to someone else, you curse the Universe for never being on your side. Meanwhile, you haven't been working very hard and the other person has. Instead of feeling happy for the other person and have it light a flame under your lazy ass to take action yourself, you choose to spend your time on your couch complaining that you have no luck, nothing ever happens for you, and you're never in the right place at the right time. F you Universe you exclaim!!

You're in a monogamous relationship and your lover is somewhere else and there's this dude/dudette and he/she's hot and you're standing under the moonlight and everything comes together and he/she moves in to kiss you and you get swept away in the moment because the force was so strong you couldn't do anything about it. Convinced that the stars aligned for this to happen and the Universe made you do it, you decide that it's not cheating so you don't tell your trusting lover at home. Your lover eventually finds out and you tell them that you were a victim of the forces of nature.

You find a wallet on the ground at a friend's house and keep it because you manifested it instead of trying to find the owner.

Going out for a night on the town without your wallet, you flirt with people you have no intention of having any sort of relationship with other than to get them to buy you drinks, dinner and cab rides. When you get home, you high five yourself for manifesting a free night out.

Feeling like the person you're with should unconditionally love you even when you're at your worst, you show them your worst more often than not and get mad when they don't like it. You tell them that they aren't very accepting and loving and that they need to work on that.

You send a really mean passive aggressive email and sign it love and light because you think that cancels out everything else you typed. Not understanding why the receiver is upset about your message, you wonder what's wrong with them. I mean, you did sign it love and light. Why can't they accept your love and light? There must be something blocking them from receiving your love and light.

Spending hours creating the perfect vision board, you sit on your ass at home and wait for the Universe to bring you all of the things, and then the Universe doesn't bring you all the things, and you blame the Universe.

You spill whiskey all over your computer when you were drunk Facebooking at 3am on a Tuesday night and you blame Mercury for being in retrograde.

You try to get into the pants of someone who's not interested in you. "How could they not want this?" you wonder. Your next move is to try to make them feel bad about themselves so you can get your way. You tell them that it's because they're not enlightened, free spirited enough, open to the magical possibilities, or living in the moment.

Your friend isn't into yoga, they eat meat, they eat gluten, they eat dairy, they eat cooked food, they eat food at all, and they don't meditate on the reg. Judging them by their non-enlightened behaviors, you talk down to them because you think you're better than them because of how spiritual you are because you pretend that you do all of those things.

If you're guilty of spiritual shenanigans, it's probably because you're a human being and you're not perfect. We've all committed these crimes, but we don't have to be incarcerated forever. Here's your get out of jail free card. Apologize to anyone you've wronged in the past with your behavior and then from this moment on, all you have to do is be radically kind to everyone and everything including yourself.

ROCK THE

MAGIC!

Come up with a list of kind things that you can do for your friends, family, community or the world. List twenty things with the goal of accomplishing at least one this week.

Tip: It's recommended that you choose things that are fun for you or that you know will leave you feeling really good. In fact, you'll probably be more successful at it and inspired to do even more.

Color this picture of your ego and decorate its surroundings. Acknowledge that everything that emerges from your ego comes from old wounds and fear so it's important to have compassion for it. For example, draw flowers, hearts, rainbows, give it a unicorn horn, or anything that means love and healing to you.

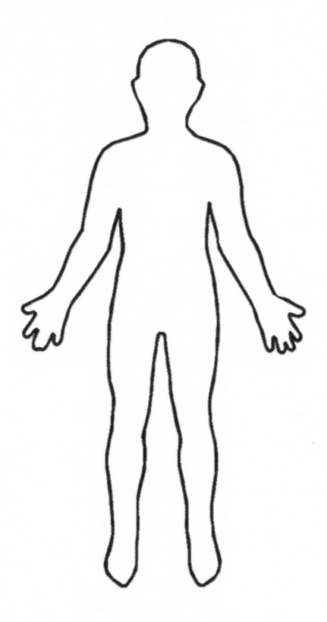

Writing Prompt

Describe a helper's high you've felt from doing something kind for someone.

Reflections

10

FORGIVE EVERYONE, FOR REALSIES

"*A hungry baby starts to cry, an old man's about to die
And all I can do is sit back and sigh, what's my problem
Ignore the problem, that's the key
Said the woman beneath the tree
If your eyes are closed, you can't see the sunrise.*"

Left Me in a Hole by Yonder Mountain String Band

I've been hurt. I've had people say and do things to me that are too horrible to even mention. When I first played with the idea of forgiving them, I thought, "Are you freakin' kidding me? How could I possibly forgive those people for the things they did? They don't deserve my forgiveness."

By me not forgiving those people, it doesn't hurt them; it hurts me. It's like I was carrying a backpack of anger everywhere I went, with no one around to help lighten the load. My bag got so heavy that I just couldn't carry it anymore. I had to put it down before it tipped me over and eventually killed me.

The UN's report titled *Forgiveness* dives into the psychological research that was done on the subject. The report explains that the studies show the importance of forgiving within your personal relationships. The research says it makes you healthier and happier.

Holding onto a grudge is bad for your health, too. It will raise your blood pressure, cause you anxiety, and can even lower your life expectancy from all the stress that goes along with it. Stop drinking green juice that you spiked with a heavy laxative hoping that the person you're mad at will shit their brains out.

I Found Compassion and Forgiveness for My Cyber Bullies. Here's How:

"Not everyone can leave their job and fuck rock stars until they get things for free, you get what you want and get to be a stupid hippy because you write and suck dick. not everyone can do that and we need doctors and people doing real work not just being groupies. some people need to return to save the world unlike you, what do you REALLY contribute?"

Those words were delivered to me responding to a Huffington Post interview I did with Mihali from the band Twiddle. This isn't the first time a little hate was thrown at me. I've been ripped apart and made fun of many times on message boards, social media, and in the comments section of my blogs, articles, and videos in very hurtful ways. I've been told things such as:

I would be much more attractive if I placed a bag over my head to cover the ugly part. My face resembled a horse's. With my cheesy writing style, I shouldn't be writing for anyone but Teen Beat. Certainly not the Huffington Post. I've got no talent and I'm just another ugly hippie trying to change the world and failing. There was even an entire thread on a message board entitled, "Taraleigh Weathers is Freakin' Annoying," where people who didn't know me bashed me hard.

It's easy to forget that there's an actual, real life person with feelings who's going to read the words written about them. Add anonymity to the equation and the word abuse gets even more out of control. Our country was built on the premise of free speech and everyone's right to their own opinion, which is awesome, but in this day and age it feels like there's no consequences when a person says whatever they want about someone, even if it's extremely hurtful.

I'm practicing the ability to never take anything personal, but since I'm not fully enlightened yet (I'm working on it), I'm not 100% immune. In the past, I used to feel every word like a knife to the back. I would allow myself to suffer from that pain for weeks on end.

Once, I put myself out into cyber land for a video contest to win a writing position and free tickets to a very prestigious music festival. We were to create videos explaining why we deserved to win. The top submissions were then brought to the public for a vote.

A couple of weeks into the competition, I found out I had made it to the top five. Yay! Shortly after, a friend alerted me that there was a thread on a message board where most of the other competitors had typed horrendously ugly words mostly directed at me. At first I was livid and wanted to go in and figuratively rip each and every one of them new buttholes. Then the next tidal wave of emotion came crashing down on me, and it was sadness. How could people be so mean? I sobbed uncontrollably. The last tear I had left in me cascaded down my flushed cheek when I was slapped upside the head with compassion for these people. There had to be a reason that they felt the need to collectively bring me down.

Instead of my original plan of 'letting them have it,' I let them know I was the woman on the receiving end of their bullying and that I, too, was a human being with feelings just like them. Their words hurt me and I wondered if they would say those things to me in real life when we met in the flesh at the festival in a couple of months.

One of the men, who deservingly ended up winning the contest, reached out to me right away. He let me know he got swept up in the competition and was threatened by me because he thought I had the best chance of beating him. His reaction was to talk smack to try to turn voters against me while at the same time attempting to lift himself up. He was so far down the competitive rabbit hole he got carried away and forgot there was a real person in those videos that deserved to win just as much as him. He professed a sincere apology which I accepted. He has never written another word rooted in hate toward another human ever again and we are now friends.

Here's another story. When I was in college I did a stint as a costumed character in a show at an amusement park. After we completed the shows every hour, we went out into the audience for a meet-and-greet. My particular character was a big flirt and I was instructed by my bosses to innocently flirt with the women who came up to me. Obeying orders, I linked arms with a woman and together we walked a couple of steps before I felt a jolting crash at the top of my costume. "Stop messing with my woman you fucking duck" I hear a man's voice exclaim as my head came crashing full speed toward the ground until my nose broke the fall as it hit the inside of my costume head.

My escort grabbed me and pulled me into the employee area where I removed the costume head to reveal my bloody nose. I immediately changed out of the costume and went out into the park to confront my bully. When he saw that I was a petite young woman, he looked mortified. He got so caught up in the situation that he forgot that I was just a person in a costume doing my job. I explained that he should be embarrassed by what he did and in the future he may want to think about the way he treats people, even if he can't see below the surface. As for his girlfriend, I told her she might want to rethink being with a man who just beat up a girl in a duck costume.

It took me a little while to forgive this man who hurt me and made me scared of people coming up and hitting me when I was in my costume. But then I thought about it. That quack beat up a woman in a duck costume! I felt sad for him that he felt like hitting me was his only option. I felt compassion for him for the poor choice he made that day, found forgiveness and was able to move on.

Ira Byock is an expert when it comes to end-of-life decisions. Dr. Byock and his research team found that two of the most important things that mattered most to those on their deathbeds was asking for forgiveness as well as letting someone know that they've been forgiven.

The good news is, you don't have to wait until you're on your deathbeds or in hospice care to do something about it. Is there someone in your life you want to ask for forgiveness from or someone you want to know that you've forgiven them? Now's the time.

Do you have someone in your life you're having trouble forgiving?

Here are five ways to forgive someone who hurt you real bad:

1. Before I received the vulgar email I shared with you at the beginning of this chapter and found that hateful thread on the message board, I was really proud of the interview I published and the video I made. After the messages, I started questioning everything before remembering that no matter

what feedback I got, positive or negative, it didn't really matter. Anything anyone says or writes is a projection of whatever is going on for them. Nothing is personal.

2. The words I read had so much hate behind them that I became aware of the suffering that the people who wrote them must be feeling, and I started to feel compassion for them. Even though I would never ever write messages like that to anyone, I'm a little like them. I've reacted in not the best ways when I felt threatened or was stricken with fear and sadness.

3. I realized something. The person who wrote me the hate mail took time out of his busy day to read the interview I wrote, click on my bio, find the link to my website, go to my website, find my contact form and write me that lovely message. It takes a lot of effort to hate on someone that much. If you think about it, it's kind of flattering.

4. My haters were totally acting like jerks, but I truly believe that deep, deep, DEEP down in their souls, they're probably not jerks. What they did wasn't acceptable or OK, but I realized they're just human beings doing their best, just like me.

5. Being on the receiving end of the hate, for a moment it felt like the easiest thing for me to do was to retreat and hide. "Screw that," I thought. "Even if it feels hard, I'm going to shine my love light all up in the face of hate." Take that, haters!

When you're online and feel the urge to write a mean comment, tear someone down or virtually bully them, remember there's a real life person with real feelings just like you who's going to read your words. Instead of using your words to spread fear and hate, use them to spread love and light. You have a superpower!!!

If you're on the receiving end of the hate, remember it's not about you. You're amazing and sometimes your awesome is just too much for people.

Need to forgive yourself for something?

It's Time to Practice Self-Forgiveness

Oftentimes it feels a billion times easier to forgive others than it does to find forgiveness for yourself. Why is that? So many reasons!!! Identifying that others are suffering and that's why they treated you poorly is clear. What if I told you the mistakes you made were a result of your own personal suffering, and you were just doing your best with what you knew at the time? Just like those you want to or have already forgiven, it doesn't make the behavior OK, but you can understand and feel compassion for them. The same goes for you.

Here's how to start forgiving yourself:

1. You're not and never will be perfect, and that's perfect. All of the mistakes you have made and all of the failures you've experienced are all a part of your journey. Learn from them so they don't keep showing up in new and different ways.
2. Don't lose sight that, at your core, you're a good person. Good people choose to do bad things sometimes. Maybe you did something that was wrong, but the truth is you're probably a good person who just happened to do a bad thing. You were more than likely doing your best with the tools and knowledge you had at the time.
3. Why did you do the things you did? Possibly you were trying to protect yourself. Or maybe you were trying to protect another person. There are a multitude of reasons why you reacted the way you did, and you know deep in your heart what the reason was.
4. This self-forgiveness work is hard stuff. Get support. Talk to someone. Start the conversation with, "The best way you can support me right now is by..."
5. If someone you loved confessed something they couldn't forgive themselves for and came to you for advice, what would you tell them? Would you help them see the path to forgiveness? You deserve to take a gander on that same path.

Suggested Listening:

The Heart of the Matter by Don Henley
Let My Love Open the Door by Pete Townshend
Sorry by Justin Bieber
Eliza by Hayley Jane and the Primates
Wings of Forgiveness India.Arie
I'm Sorry by Brenda Lee

ROCK THE

MAGIC!

Write down the names of people you want to forgive.

Next to their names write down why you have compassion for them, and then simply write, "I forgive you."

Bonus points: Rip out this page and ceremonially burn it.

Writing Prompt

Write a letter to yourself. Start with: I forgive myself for _____ because _____.

Reflections

11

MAKE SWEET MOVES

"It's so important that we keep pushing forth thru the darkness
Like the phoenix we must rise thru the fire with vengeance
Cause they'll try to keep you down with their lies and their nonsense
Don't you listen to them child
Come with us
It'll all make sense"

The Light by Kat Wright & the Indomitable Soul Band

The telephone was ringing, so I handed it to Liz. Just kidding. If you don't get why I would joke about handing the phone to someone named Liz, listen to the song by Phish called *Wolfman's Brother*. But for real, the phone was actually ringing and it felt like my heart was going to burst out of my chest from the anticipation of the reaction my best friend was sure to give me after I shared my big news with her. Picking up the phone before she had a chance to say hello, I blurted out, "I finally figured out what I want to do with my life! I'm going to be a bla bla bla (insert latest declaration)."

"Oh" she said with way less excitement in her voice than I prepared myself for. She continued, "Tara, you know you have to do bla bla bla (insert truth) and it's really hard work." My hopes and dreams immediately felt like they were being flushed down the drain.

But my bestie had a point. This was not the first time I declared with gusto to her and the world something I was going to do, and after considering the work it took to actually do it, bailing and moving on to the next declaration.

The times I did start to actually do something and an obstacle popped up, I made up a million and one excuses about why that dream didn't pan out. Quicker than a blink of an eye, I moved on and was scheming up a new and exciting dream to talk about.

Suffering from a serious case of action-a-phobia perpetuated by my fear of failure, this ailment caused me to be the most epic of all epic dreamers. The high I felt speaking about all the amazing ideas I had, the things I was going to do and accomplish, and all the fabulous places I was going to travel to was addicting. When it came to actually doing something about making those dreams become a reality, I got scared, and it paralyzed me.

I thought that living in a constant state of dreaming was my solution to find happiness, but it was an illusion. Not accepting reality and choosing a fantasy world instead, I felt a false sense of joy and satisfaction that never lasted very long. I was living one big fat stinky lie and it was starting to kill me from the inside out.

The pesky voice in my head that was telling me that I couldn't follow through with anything, that voice I listened to for so long, was speaking up to try to protect me from pain. In my younger years, I went for a dream and it was abruptly ripped out from under my feet. Secretly I was terrified it would happen again, which is why I was subconsciously sabotaging myself.

I Accomplished a Dream and Lost It.

Twirling around in my bedroom growing up, I dreamt about one day becoming a professional dancer. After begging and pleading with my parents, they enrolled me in dance classes. From the very first moment, I was hooked

For the next 25 years, I wore a leotard and tights almost daily. Most of my time was devoted to becoming a master of my craft. Free weekend time was pretty much non-existent. I had to decline many invitations to parties, and I rarely got to just hang out with friends and relax after school.

Nothing could deter me from pursuing my dream. Not when I gave up my social life, and not when I was told that I was too fat/too short/ had the wrong body type to ever become a successful dancer. Those sacrifices and discouraging messages could have sent me to quit and toss my leotards into a river, but they didn't. Instead, a fire was lit inside me to prove everyone wrong and succeed.

I decided to take this thing to the next level. Taking sweet action on a daily basis and working my tail off, people were finally starting to take notice. I won many national awards, earned a degree in dance from Arizona State University, went on to dance professionally in New York City for a number of dance companies, and even became a cheerleader for a professional basketball team. It was all happening and I was so proud of myself.

And then the magic carpet got ripped out from under my feet. One of the worst things that ever happened to me, up until that point, was very publicly shown to thousands of people on a Jumbotron live at a sold out professional basketball game. After a traumatic fall during the halftime performance, I struggled to get to my feet unsuccessfully as the crowd gasped in horror. Panicked, I started to crawl off the court in order to avoid becoming dancer roadkill. A man in shining armor came to my rescue, scooped me up and brought me to the team's doctor for a prognosis. In a few minutes I went from being the star of the team to suffering a knee injury that crushed my dance career. To say I was devastated is a gross understatement.

I was a dancer. Now I can't dance. What was I supposed to do with myself and who the heck am I?

My subconscious had a master plan I wasn't keen to and it worked for many years. A bunch of walls were being built to protect me from something like that ever happening again. The plan was working so well that I secretly decided I wouldn't actually follow through with anything ever again.

Spoiler alert! It didn't work.

I knew something had to change, but my damn nagging thoughts were doing everything in their power to keep me from taking any risks. After all, I had spent most of my adult life listening to those thoughts and giving them all the power. I was aware they wouldn't just go away overnight, so what's a girl to do? Instead of trying with all my might to forcefully evict them, I tried something new. I thanked them for their service and wished them well.

"Thank you for stepping up to protect me from making the same mistakes, but this time I'm willing to take the chance even if it means getting hurt again. You are free to go. Good bye!"

241

And like magic, it all happened. But it wasn't magic at all.

Once I got out of my own way I realized that even though I'm not a professional dancer in the preconceived societal expectation of what a dancer is, I'm a dancer. You know why? Because I still dance! I use my dance skills almost daily as a way to get out of my head and into my body and heart so I feel inspired to take sweet action. Dancers and non-dancers alike are taught many of the techniques I've learned throughout the years at the retreats I host and workshops I present to do just that. So you might even say that I never lost my dream of becoming a professional dancer. It just looks way different than I thought it would.

How I Made The Dream of Writing this Book a Reality

The idea of writing a book has been sitting on my back burner for years. Talking about it was extremely enjoyable because I felt high when people got really excited for me. What scared me shitless was the daunting task of actually doing it. My writing mentor Suzanne Boothby once shared with me that a writer's greatest fear is looking at a blank page and having all day to write on it. Add to that the crippling thoughts in my head that questioned my ability, paired with the fear that no one actually cared what I had to say, left me feeling like I was unsuccessfully attempting to swim in a vat of molasses.

Years went by, but I couldn't shake the dream out of my head.

Having stepped up my yoga game, I'd learned to breathe through challenging situations, and I realized that maybe the crazy hard task of writing a book wouldn't be so impossible after all. If I somehow found a way to feel good when my body was twisted up like a pretzel while balancing on my head, I could more than likely find comfort anywhere!

I decided I was going to do it for real this time, and check it out... I did it. Go me!

So how did I do it? Let me use my words to tell you.

I started. I put my pen to paper, wrote a few words and I didn't stop for a couple of years.

I created inspiring playlists. Whenever I felt stuck or just needed a little more inspiration, I listened to music. I had a couple of playlists that had my favorite songs on them that would always, without fail, get me moving. Also, Holly Bowling. Trust me.

I found a writing buddy. My friend Morella, who was also writing a book, committed to holding me accountable and I was to do the same for her. We made writing dates where we not only wrote our sweet asses off, but we ran ideas past each other, read excerpts out loud and gave and received feedback to each other. The thought of backing out came to me a couple of times, but I knew Morella would bitch slap me if I did, so I kept truckin.

I tackled the big tasks in tiny chunks. Every time I sat down to write, I set a timer for twenty minutes and got down to business. When the timer went off, I took a break and decided if I wanted to continue for another twenty.

I left all my judgements at the door. Something that was threatening to hold me back was the fear that people would think my writing was stupid, not important, bad and annoying. Another fear I had was vulnerably sharing my dark side and having it change others' opinions of me. Instead of writing to the criticizing masses, I wrote pretending that no one would ever read it.

I visualized the outcome. I felt what it would feel like to walk into a bookstore and see my book as a featured best seller. Picking it up off the shelf, I felt the crisp white pages as they flipped past my fingers. I put my nose to the page and took a deep breath in, smelling the fresh ink. As I placed the book back where I found it, I admired the beautifully designed cover. I pictured the faces of the people who read it and were inspired by it. I imagined the conversations they had about my book with their friends.

I felt all the feels. Tears of joy welled up in my eyes when the first chapter was finally written. Shortly after when I accidentally erased it, losing it to the black hole of cyberspace, I felt so angry that I gave my pillow an epic punching. I leaked awesome out of my eyes when I read a passage to a crowd, who were so connected to my words, that water trickled down their cheeks. I screamed bloody murder when I found out that after three revisions, the un-proofread transcript almost accidentally went to print. Shortly afterward, I felt an overwhelming sense of gratitude that it didn't actually go to print so I could fix it.

I surrendered to the flow. It's a habit for me to try to force things to happen when I want them to instead of allowing it all to unfold when it's supposed to. I had to let that go and trust that Divine timing is where it's at.

Heart Something Daily

It's time to start implementing the unique gifts you've been hiding into your daily life. It's scary to go for it for real, but lying on your deathbed knowing you were too much of a coward to try is even more terrifying. Some lucky ducks are born knowing what their gifts are and never forget. For others, like me, it takes much longer. Instead of trying with all your might to think it out of you, feel it out instead. What do you heart doing? Or what did you used to heart doing as a child?

Don't get sucked into the 'I must find my purpose pressure cooker' and drive yourself bonkers. Remember, all you have to do is be the wildest authentic expression of yourself and apply it to your current situation. And do it every single day in everything you do.

For example, Trey Anastasio from the band Phish is a gifted guitar player, but if he sat on his couch all day and played video games instead of practicing guitar as much as possible, he wouldn't be the rockstar he is today, and we would be denied of his gift.

Don't be selfish and deny the world of your gift.

Daily, consistent actions create sweet results and you'll become an expert in a small amount of time. Allowing space for this action daily will make small improvements quickly turn into massive ones.

To pick your own personal daily habit to hone, ask what could you do on a daily basis that improves your life, unleashes your creativity, and you realistically could accomplish doing once a day.

Some examples are spending an hour practicing guitar, doing a handstand, writing for fifteen minutes, adding green leafy veggies to one meal, drinking a large glass of water, practicing yoga, meditating for five minutes, chanting your mantras, dancing, singing one song, making art, or maybe taking three deep, conscious breaths.

Pick one action. Once you finish doing it, put big red heart on your calendar. If you use an online calendar, simply use a heart emoji. Each day, after you've completed your task, you will add another heart.

If you fell off your unicorn, aren't doing your daily task and are having trouble getting back in the saddle, it doesn't mean that all you've done up to this point was meaningless and that you should throw in the towel and give up.

When it comes to creating new habits, the human brain is a fascinating thing to study. Habits are like raging rivers in your head. The longer you've had the habit, the stronger the river rages. When you start a new habit, it's like filling a bucket of water from the raging river and dumping it out next to the river expecting it to rage as hard as the original river. Every so often, it's human nature to get swept away by the bigger/stronger river. When this happens, get up, shake the water off of you like a wet puppy, and pick up your bucket and try again. Eventually, you'll create your own raging river for the behavior you want and the old river will dry up.

New habits take time.

I heart you.

Suggested Listening:

Learning to Fly by Tom Petty
You Make My Dreams Come True by Hall and Oates
Dreamer by The Head and the Heart
Do it For the Love by Michael Franti & Spearhead
Keep Going by The Revivalists
Do It Daily by Martin Sexton
Tahoe Tweezer by Holly Bowling

ROCK THE

MAGIC!

What is one thing that you can do this week (because actions are like dominos) that will set you in motion to rock your life?

Is it calling a friend? Is it setting up your date with your Life Sponsor? Is it checking out that class or program you've been thinking about doing that will add sparkle to your career? Is it looking at ticket prices for the trip you've always talked about taking so you can start saving? Or is it writing the outline of the book you've always wanted to write?

Writing Prompts

If you had a magic wand and could use it to be living your dream life right now, what would your life look like?

What's stopping you?

What are you going to do about it?

Reflections

12

ROCK YOUR LIFE

"She knows nothing at all about life
She knows everything about living"

Moth by Moe.

Overwhelmed by the beautiful music that was coming from the festival stage, the people dancing all around her, and safety she felt to truly be the wildest expression of her authentic self, her glitter covered eyes filled with tears of joy. "I feel so spiritual and connected to the oneness of the planet right now," she said.

Her friend responded in all seriousness, "My toothbrush is just as spiritual as this festival, and I feel connected to the oneness every time I brush my teeth."

Cracking up, without saying another word, they looked into each other's wise eyes with a knowing that they were both correct. Music festivals are basically churches for live music lovers. Just a taste of their magic is enough to take any fanatic's breath away. Feeling spiritual and connected to everything when you're grooving on a field, soaking in everything, surrounded by others who are all there for the same purpose, is much easier than when you're at home in the middle of a work crisis.

Spending years trying to find it, I looked everywhere I could think of. I've searched the planet for it, looked to friends for it, tried to find it in lovers, scoured the festival grounds, and purchased possessions to try get it with no avail; I hoped to receive it from the wisdom I learned from my teachers, hired coaches to help me see it, went to so many festivals, read all the books to hopefully awaken something, and spent thousands of dollars on spiritual tools, but it eluded me. I did all the things that you're supposed to do and some things worked for awhile, until they didn't. On my epic quest for true happiness, I was so busy looking everywhere outside of myself for it that I totally missed the point. No person, place, band, or thing can make me truly happy for the long haul. "Where was the freakin happiness lurking?" I wondered. Oh right! It was within me the whole entire gosh darn time!

It's like the person who blames where they live for their lack of happiness. They move to paradise with the expectation that all their problems will melt away. But they don't go away and everything gets even worse than before. Blaming paradise for not giving them what they needed they move elsewhere and start the whole cycle again. The key that's missing is their happiness doesn't solely rely on where they live because paradise (or hell) lives in them, meaning location is only a tiny factor.

However connected you feel at whatever your version of a music festival is, there's no reason why you can't feel even a smidge of that way every single day in every situation. Even brushing your teeth can feel magical because the magic is everywhere and in everything. It's even in you, you beautiful beast.

Have you ever been around someone who was so clearly living with the intent to love everything and everyone? It's like they're a love magnet and it's impossible to not be affected in some way. Even when you're going through the hardest times and things are so bad that you can't see the light, they'll see it for you. Enveloping you with pure unconditional love before you know what hit you, you'll be changed for the better. At the time you might not even know what they did for you, but you'll realize what happened later. This type of person doesn't take themselves too seriously, but at the same time, they're not joking around either. Know the kind of person I'm talking about? There are many of you out there, but this is how Phish's drummer Jon Fishman described Col. Bruce Hampton shortly after he passed away on stage at his 70th birthday celebration.

Col. Bruce chose to live life that way (with the intent to unconditionally love everything and everyone) and you can make that same choice.

It takes a shift in your brain to starting living that way and that's what this book was all about. I didn't go from a shy second grader who was afraid to speak up or a teenager who was embarrassed to cry and had temper tantrums or a twenty something in an abusive relationship or an injured dancer in her thirties who didn't know what to do with herself to the sparkly unicorn I am today.

It took a boat load of work to get here, I messed up a zillion times, and had many things I tried to do fail. Even on the days when things got so bad and it felt so hard I seriously contemplated throwing in the towel and giving up, but I didn't. Instead I picked up the towel I had thrown on the ground, wiped away my tears with it, and put one foot in front of the other because it was all I had in me to do at the time. Those pivotal moments with all the darkness and anguish were so magical and made me into the person I am today. Looking back now, I'm so grateful they happened.

I wish I had this book when I was too scared to let the wildest expression of my authentic self out. But you're a lucky individual. You have this book! And you read it. You're amazing in my book and this is my book so it's obviously the truth.

Moving forward, make it your mission to be the person who inspires others to see that even the things that seem impossible, are in fact possible. Shine your light so bright that it lights up the worlds' of the people around you. Be a fucking inspiration. Be you.

One major side effect of this book is erectile dysfunction. Just kidding! It's that you'll fall in love with someone very special. YOU! And just when you think you have reached your limit of self-love, you'll find that you can take your love to the next level. Give yourself the key to your place. Move in together. Live happily ever after. If something or someone comes in and tries to threaten your love and you forget who you are, this book and all the tools in it are always there for your use unless someone steals it from you. In that case, hopefully they'll read it and will learn that they shouldn't steal and you can go out and purchase another copy.

If all else fails, find a baby, puppy or kitten as soon as possible and look at him or her. Finding it impossible to feel anything but unconditional love for all that squishy adorable cuteness, remember you were once a baby, too. People looked at you the same way. Today, you're a big ol' baby deserving of just as much love. Try to tell that baby that they're not loveable. I dare you. It's impossible!

Rocking your life has little to do with the past or the future and everything to do with the right here, right now. Every year on the first of January, I come up with an intention. A couple of years ago, my mantra was to find the magic in all situations. At a concert, I found it was simple, but in other circumstances it was more challenging.

Grieving the death of a loved one, getting stuck in traffic when I was running late, and holding a really difficult pose in yoga class all put my intention to the test. Was it possible to find magic even in the most tragic and uncomfortable of situations? At first I couldn't always find it. Keeping an open mind and repeating my mantra daily, eventually the magic would reveal itself. Feel free to borrow my mantra for as long as you want.

All my personal stories throughout the book and the lessons that were taught contain all the tools you need to rock your own life. Consciously infuse live music magic into your everyday experience, get high, believe that magic is normal, achieve self-care superhero status, slay the time and energy vampires, take the highway to the awesome zone, become a manifesting unicorn, feel all the feels, stop being an ass, forgive everyone for realsies, make sweet moves, and before you know it, your life will be officially rocked.

Be your own festival and life will feel like a festival.

It's all happening and you earned the lead in the play of your life. There's no understudy, although there may be someone lurking in the wings waiting for you to fall so they can take your place. Whatever. Even if you fall, it's all a part of the show and you're irreplaceable anyway. No one can play this part as good as you. How cool is that? In this production you get to fly over the crowd like the actor gets to do in Peter Pan because you're a magical Jedi. Get ready for the groupies because you've officially achieved rock star status. Grab life by the unicorn horn, close this book, get out there and rock your life.

Suggested Listening:

Life's Been Good by Joe Walsh
Turn on Your Love Lights by The Righteous Brothers
I Can See Clearly Now by Jimmy Cliff
I'm Free by the Soup Dragons
Be Well by Jesse Taylor
Hurt No More by Aquarium Rescue Unit

ROCK THE MAGIC!

Get out there and rock your life.

The end.

Just kidding!

It's just the beginning and it's ALL happening.

Warning!!!

This book will self-destruct in

5, 4, 3, 2...

Haha! I think I'm funny.

I would never let this book self-destruct because it's meant to be read over and over again and shared with someone you think would benefit from it. My hope is that it lives on forever and gets passed down through the generations.

I'm having a really hard time saying goodbye to you.

So I'm not going to say goodbye.

Instead, I'm going to say,

"Until we meet again."

I'm looking forward to that day.

See you dancing on the
concert field!

The end.

For real this time.

The book is ending, but the sweet life has just begun.

Rage it!!!

I love you!

ABOUT THE AUTHOR

Taraleigh is a wild sequin-and-feather wearin' live music fanatic residing in Vermont. If you find a pile of dirt, sand and glitter in her place, it's what's left after she exploded from the excitement that you're reading her book.

Literally dancing her way through life, (as a competitive dancer in her school years, earning a BFA in dance studies and choreography from Arizona State University and becoming a professional dancer and tumbler for the NBA) she found herself happiest when dancing to live music.

It was at festivals where she let her freak flag fly and became inspired to become a catalyst of more magic in the real world. To deepen her studies she attended the Institute for Integrative Nutrition, where she came a health and lifestyle coach. Quickly, she realized that live music fans were her most favorite people to work with. After quite the journey, she launched the Rock Your Life brand which includes coaching, leading retreats with musicians for their fans, workshops, speaking engagements, writing for publications such as the HuffPost and Relix, and this book. Taraleigh and her husband Dan run a retreat center in Vermont on a farm, called This Wonderful Place. She hopes to see you there!

Taraleigh is available for speaking engagements, festivals, and workshops. Find out more at www.taraleighlovesyou.com

Rock your mind, body and soul before, during and after the festival by getting sparkles, smoothies, & rock-n-roll delivered to your inbox directly from Taraleigh. Sign up at www.taraleighlovesyou.com

BOOK CLUB QUESTIONS:

1. What was your initial reaction to the book? Did it hook you right away, or did it take some time to get into?

2. Which of the 12 chapters resonated the most with you and why? Consciously Infuse the Live Music Magic Into Your Everyday Experience, Get High, Magic is Normal, Achieve Self-Care Superhero Status, Slay the Time and Energy Vampires, Take the Highway to the Awesome Zone, Become a Manifesting Unicorn, Feel All the Feels, Stop Being an Ass, Forgive Everyone, For Realsies, Make Sweet Moves, or Rock Your Life.

3. Which lesson was the most important or relevant to your own experience? Why?

4. What was your favorite Taraleigh-ism?

5. Share a story when you experienced a miracle similar to the ones shared in Chapter Three.

6. What's holding you back from living your dream life?

7. What's your self-care kryptonite?

8. How do you think Taraleigh handled her cyberbullies in Chapter Ten? How do you handle the bullies in your life?

9. In Chapter Six, Taraleigh talks about the dreaded Universal Bitch Slap. Discuss a time you've received one.

10. What action do you want to take in your life that would make Taraleigh proud?

GRATITUDE

I am grateful for:

Everyone who was ever mean to me, because you were my greatest teachers. My husband Dan, who is never mean to me, and continues to show me unconditional, forever-growing, deep, sexy, supportive love. My parents and sister, who have lovingly pushed me to be the best me that I can be, even though I can be quite annoying sometimes. My nieces and nephews Zoey, Josie, Ryan, Natalia, Devon, Rocco, Anthony and all the other kiddos in my life who are constantly challenging me to play harder and not take life so seriously. My beloved Grammy Helen, who told the best stories about laundry I've ever heard in my life (and who is totally responsible for my storytelling talent), who never thought she was old (even in her 90's), and made friends with everyone she came in contact with. My in-laws, who accepted me into their wild karaoke-singing family with open arms and loved me from day one.

My manager Alexandra Dempsey who is the wind beneath my wings. Dobra Tea and Caitlin from Sangha Studio, for giving me the most beautiful, warm physical space to write this book. Holly Bowling for providing the perfect soundtrack to write to. Rose, my astro-mama, for her fabulous editing skills and loyal support. Morella, my writing buddy, for holding me accountable to get shit done and for totally crushing the Rock the Magic sections. Thank you Jasmine for being a word, hashtag and photo fairy. Maia and Al for making sure my words sound right. My mom, for being my fairy grammar mother. Book angel Suzanne Boothby, for igniting my written voice. My unicorn soul sisters (aka my Life Sponsors) Cora, Suz, and Shells, who shone a light on all the parts of me and love them. My book launch team who took time out of their busy lives to give me really great feedback and who brought the book to the place I wanted it to go. You all saw what I couldn't.

Joshua Rosenthal from the Institute for Integrative Nutrition, for picking me out of a crowd to let me know I was going to do something great one day, when I didn't see it at all. Jonathan Schwartz, for listening to the craziness I spewed out of my mouth and seeing the diamond in what I shared. The entire Zappos and Life is Beautiful family for loving my brand of weird and supporting me in so many ways. Oteil Burbridge, for writing the foreword and inspiring me with his ability to trust in the unknown while fully embracing life and living in the awesome zone. I'm a member of the O-Zone for life! Ryan Montbleau, for his miracle story and being my first retreat partner in crime. Thank you for putting your whole soul into your music and inspiring me to do that with my writing. Hayley Jane for being a courageous, powerful badass of a woman and bringing that out in me. Joel Cummins, Jessica Burbridge, Erin Campos, Marinda Righter, Stephen Kiernan, Morella Devost, and Stephanie Spivak for their miracle story contributions. Jeffrey Rhodes, for taking my Healthy Hippie newsletter and turning it into print for the first time. You saw the magic in my words and I'm so grateful. Judd Lamphere, for your photography skills and for that beer we shared while heartstorming the title of this book. Britt Nemeth, for her moral support and epic photography. My friends and family, who know I'm crazy and love me anyway. Thank you Bob Shultz for rocking a last minute photo shoot that produced my author pic. Live music and festivals, for being my happy place and giving me a safe space to let my freak flag fly. The people who trigger me—because of them I continue to grow, evolve, and move to the next level of awesome.

You, my readers—thank YOU for taking the time out of your busy life to read my book. And myself, because "Dude! I wrote a book." Without myself, I never could have written this book. Go me!

Made in United States
North Haven, CT
25 August 2022

23178099R00189